Heidi I. Stull

The Evolution of the Autobiography from 1770–1850

A Comparative Study and Analysis

PETER LANG

New York · Berne · Frankfurt am Main

Library of Congress Cataloging in Publication Data

Stull, Heidi I., 1930–
The Evolution of the Autobiography from 1770–1850.

(American University Studies. Series III, Comparative Literature; v. 11)
Bibliography: p.
1. Autobiography.   I. Title.   II. Series.
CT25.S78   1984   809'.93592   84-47683
ISBN 0-8204-0133-1
ISSN 0724-1445

CIP-Kurztitelaufnahme der Deutschen Bibliothek

Stull, Heidi I.:
The Evolution of the Autobiography from 1770–
1850: a Comparative Study and Analysis / Heidi
I. Stull. – New York; Berne; Frankfurt
am Main: Lang, 1985.
    (American University Studies: Ser. 3,
    Comparative Literature; Vol. 11)
    ISBN 0-8204-0133-1

NE: American University Studies / 03

© Peter Lang Publishing, Inc., New York 1985

Printed by Lang Druck, Inc., Liebefeld/Berne (Switzerland)

The Evolution of the Autobiography from 1770–1850

American University Studies

Series III
Comparative Literature

Vol. 11

PETER LANG
New York · Berne · Frankfurt am Main

To my husband
whose love, patience,
and encouragement made
this work possible

ACKNOWLEDGEMENTS

I owe thanks to many persons at John Carroll University, Case Western Reserve University, and Kent State University who, at different times and in varying degrees, enriched, inspired, and prepared me for the writing of this work. My heartfelt thanks go to Miss Ruth Carsten, John Carroll University, whose guidance, devotion, and hard work laid the foundation for any success I met with in the course of my studies.

Professor Martin Nurmi of Kent State University introduced me with contagious enthusiasm to the multifaceted and dynamic aspects of British Romantic literature. I am also most grateful to Professor Spengemann for providing me with a copy of his "Saint Augustine and the Problem of Romantic Autobiography." My very special gratitude goes to Professors William Hildebrand and Helmut Germer of Kent State University. Their valuable advice and guidance were a source of endless encouragement and certainly enhanced this work in many ways.

Last, but not least, thanks are due to Professor Richard Clancey, whose encouragement led to the publication of this work, and to John Carroll University for its support.

TABLE OF CONTENT

PREFACE

Autobiographical writings have always played an important role in the literary tradition of Western Civilization. Though always eagerly read by the general public, they have proven of particular interest to the scholar of literature, history, sociology, or psychology. Yet, though a number of anthologies of the most outstanding autobiographies and confessions have been published and several individual works, such as the *Confessions* of Saint Augustine or Jean-Jacques Rousseau, Cellini's *Autobiography*, or Montaigne's *Essays*, have received considerable attention, comparatively few and only rather tentative efforts have been made to examine the genre as such. This study is an attempt to examine one period in the evolution of this much neglected genre and to pinpoint the works and those elements in them which inaugurated this evolution. At the same time it tries to clarify some of the confusion that surrounds the classification of autobiographical writings in general.

The existing abundance of autobiographical writings imposes a spatial and material limitation upon any critical in-depth approach. This study, therefore, will concentrate on the period and the works which, according to my premises, brought about the most fundamental changes. It will examine these changes which are so decisive, so profound that they jeopardize the very validity of the autobiography's integrity as a genre. The period will include the years 1770-1850. Under scrutiny are primarily autobiographical works by Rousseau, Wordsworth, Goethe, De Quincey, and Grillparzer. Representative works were chosen from English, French, and German authors in order to show that the new developments in autobiography were not confined to any one national literature, but that they were rather the result of a new consciousness, a new mode of thought and sensibility, generally known as Romanticism.

Despite considerable disagreement among scholars as to the exact definition of the autobiographical genre, this study postulates the existence of a coherent genre comprising confessions, *Selbstbe-*

kenntnisse, autobiographies, and similar writings which — though by their very nature unique and highly individualistic — unfold in retrospect and in all sincerity the experiences and events which shaped the author's personality, his spiritual, intellectual, and/or artistic development. It is important to note that the demand for sincerity and truth implies by no means the representation of purely factual data, but rather the truth according to the author's experience. Preliminary studies showed that most autobiographical writings prior to 1770 could safely be included in a genre of such definition. The analyses of the chosen works will show why and how the genre undergoes a severe identity crises, making it henceforth impossible to accommodate all future so-called autobiographical writings under one single definition without destroying the very concept of the autobiography. New developments in literature (especially the emergence of the novel) and new trends in philosophy and aesthetics had ushered in a new era reflective of a new consciousness. Four of the five chosen autobiographies either herald or reflect these new trends and developments. As a direct consequence of these works, the autobiographical genre evolves from that period on into distinctly different branches:

a) the classical or conventional autobiography (as in the case of Grillparzer), in which the author's sole concern is to present the story of his life as factually and "objectively" as possible;

b) "Poetry and Truth" — Goethe and Wordsworth — in which the factual autobiographical experience is sacrificed or at least subjected to the artistic intent; and

c) the autobiographical novel (often referred to as Künstlerroman) — Goethe's *Werther*, Rousseau's *Nouvelle Héloïse* — in which an occasional glimpse of the author's personal experience is discernible, but which, because of its primarily fictional character, must be relegated to the genre of the novel.

All three branches have found numerous adherents and continue to flourish in our day so that we cannot consider this division to be a temporary deviation of an established genre. Rather, the phenomenon of the 1800s, through its ready acceptance and imitation, has become the commonplace a century later.

This study consists of six parts. Chapter one presents an overview and a definition of the autobiographical genre valid and acceptable until roughly 1770. It assesses its importance and popularity within the literary tradition. Chapters two through five give an overview of Rousseau's *Confessions*, Wordsworth's *The Prelude*, De Quincey's *Confessions of An English Opium-Eater*, and Goethe's *Dichtung und Wahrheit*. The examination brings out the innovations contributed by the individual authors and/or the expansion their contributions caused to the autobiographical genre. Chapter six, the conclusion, includes a methodological comparison of Grillparzer's *Autobiography* with the aforementioned works.

Jean-Jacques Rousseau, the first autobiographer to secularize the confession, reveals in his work a revolutionary, novel mode of thought and life. Reverie and introspection and his adamant insistence on his own particular individuality had shaped his life. These very same elements determine the scope and character of his autobiography.

If Rousseau's concern had been focused on the antagonism between civilized society and the interest of the individual, Wordsworth's preoccupations were centered on the realm of mental growth and poetry. Step by step his protagonist advances from the temporal toward the eternal. The individual transcends time and place to attain universal consciousness. The growth of the mind — in particular that of the creative artist — not the discomforts of the flesh, constitutes the essence of Wordsworth's work. To represent his growth and upward surge in a poetically flawless crescendo, he uses not only autobiographical data, but without hesitation subjects and modifies such data to his artistic intent. His prime concern was the writing of a work of art which he chose to base upon autobiographical experience.

De Quincey's *Confessions of An English Opium Eater*, while reiterating matter-of-factly many a theme presented as a manifesto some fifty years earlier in Jean-Jacques Rousseau's work and taken up by nearly every romantic writer throughout the Continent and the British Isles, is of considerable interest in the evolution of autobiography as well as of modern man. He pushes both human experience and the autobiographical genre to their extreme limits. Man in his search for expanded consciousness cannot go beyond De Quincey's experiences. Nor can the autobiography be extended any farther without losing its identity as a genre. This strange admixture of reality and fantasia-fairy tale-science fiction-combination brings the genre perilously close to such purely fictional confessions as Hogg's *Confessions of a Justified Sinner.* The protagonist's opium-induced visions expanded his consciousness far beyond J.-J. Rousseau's innocent reveries, but, while Wordsworth's expanded consciousness led to serenity and peace of mind, it brought De Quincey agony, torment, and fears of madness.

The aged Goethe, whose life had become synonymous with poetry (he repeatedly stated that he transformed automatically every image, every experience into poetry), recognized the poet's violation of the autobiographical genre. The very title of his work — *Poetry and Truth* — calls the reader's attention to this existing dichotomy caused by the poet's dual and at times conflicting ambitions: to render an accurate account of his life and to produce at the same time a work of art. In Goethe's as in Wordsworth's case, artistic considerations outweigh those of facticity.

Grillparzer, finally, despite Rousseau, Wordsworth, and Goethe, continues to write autobiography as it had been written throughout the ages: lucid, factual, and sincere, without ulterior motives or preoccupations other than those of wanting to record the facts of his life. I have included his work in this study in order to show that conventional autobiography as it had been written by Cellini, Montaigne, Jung-Stilling, and countless others, was by no means dead.

CHAPTER I

THE AUTOBIOGRAPHY AND THE
WESTERN LITERARY TRADITION

More than two centuries ago some writers and scholars recognized the intrinsic value of autobiographical materials not only for the student of literature, but also for the historian, the sociologist, and the psychologist. As early as 1796 and 1799 a collection of autobiographies was published by David Christian Seybold at the suggestion of J.G. Herder.[1] Possibly the most voluminous of these early collections was published in London during the years 1826-1833 for the reader's instruction and amusement.[2] Following the publication of J.-J. Rousseau's tremendously popular *Confessions* (i.e., from the late eighteenth century on) the publication of autogiographical writings assumed ever greater importance. The writing of autobiography in our century has taken on such proportions that anybody who considers himself to be somebody (and this assumption does not necessarily have to be confirmed by popular vote), or who, while already

1 *Selbstbiographien berühmter Männer*. Herder in a letter dated May 1790 sums up autobiographies as follows: „Sie sind wahre Vermächtnisse der Sinnesart denkwürdiger Personen, Spiegel der Zeitumstände, in denen sie lebten, und eine praktische Rechenschaft, was sie aus solchen und aus sich selbst gemacht haben und worin sie sich und ihre Zeit versäumt haben."
Karl Phillip Moritz (1757-1792) insisted on the importance of such writings for the psychological and moral analysis of man and published in *Magazin für Erfahrungsseelenlehre* (established in 1783) a considerable number of autobiographies.
   cf. Georg Misch, *Geschichte der Autobiographie*, vol. 4, second half, Frankfurt/M., G. Schulte-Bulmke-Verlag, 1969, p. 784.
2 This collection consisted of thirty-four volumes and was published under the title: *Autobiography. A Collection of the Most Instructive and Amusing Lives Ever Published, Written by the Parties Themselves.*
   N.B. Throughout this study all quotations within the text are given in English, quotations in the footnotes are given in the original.

well established in the limelights, hopes to replenish his bank account, will write the story of his life, assuming quite correctly that the reading public, basically not very different from that of the eighteenth century, is eager to buy anything that promises some choice tidbits spiced liberally with scandal, sensation, and a trace of paranoia. As a consequence the library shelves today harbor such confessions as that of a thug,[3] of a mask,[4] of a people lover,[5] of a puzzled parson,[6] of a disloyal European,[7] of a European intellectual,[8] of a poet,[9] of a violinist,[10] and myriads more. Though often the title alludes to the profession, character, vice, or virtue of the narrator, it does little to enlighten the reader as far as the type of the work itself is concerned, i.e., whether it is a conventional autobiography, a work of fiction, or maybe an autobiographical novel. Frequently these writings are of very little literary value, yet they all seem to appeal to a substantial number of readers who seem neither too discriminating, nor too demanding of the presented subject matter. A prefacing assurance of the author or the "editor" that the work is, indeed, a factual account generally satisfies the reader and often assures a work of fiction, published in the guise of an autobiography or confession, a sales volume comparable to any authentic autobiography.

3 Taylor Meadows, *The Confessions of a Thug*, London and New York, Oxford University Press, 1916.
4 Mishima Yukio (pseud. Hiraoka Kimilte), *The Confessions of a Mask*, tr. Meredith Weatherby, New York, New Directions, 1958.
5 Paul Ritchie, *The Confessions of a People Lover*, London, Calder & Boyars, 1967.
6 Charles Fiske, *The Confessions of a Puzzled Parson*, Freeport, Books for Libraries Press, 1968.
7 Jan Myrdal, *The Confessions of a Disloyal European*, New York, Pantheon Books, 1968.
8 Franz Schoenberner, *The Confessions of a European Intellectual*, New York, Macmillan Company, 1946.
9 Paul Verlaine, *Confessions d'un poète*, New York, Philosophical Library, 1950.
10 Th. L. Phipson, *The Confessions of a Violinist*, Philadelphia, J.B. Lippincott Company, 1902.

16

The reader's avidity for autobiographical writings is not a recent development. Accounts of personal experiences had attracted considerable numbers of readers as early as the beginning of the seventeenth century. Lives and travel narratives were then very much in vogue. In the course of the eighteenth century private travels and expeditions to foreign and often exotic lands and continents had attained unprecedented numbers, and those people who had remained behind were eagerly devouring the descriptions which reached them about foreign people, strange mores, and the exotic marvels of botanical and zoological discoveries.[11] It is, therefore, not surprising to see a substantial number of novels (a genre which was rapidly gaining popularity) based on such travel accounts or lives. Many an author, quick to realize the importance of reader preference and reaction, therefore, published his strictly fictional narrative in the first person singular. Some of these authors had no intention of deceiving the reading public, for their titles clearly indicate that narrator and author are two different individuals. Their intention rather seems to have been the establishment of a solid and intimate relationship between reader and narrator.[12]

Other authors, however, went to great lengths to explain in tedious prefaces how such and such a secret or adventure was entrusted to their care by a dying friend. Others, still more deceptive, entitled their creation *The Confessions of ...* or the *Memoirs of ...*, publishing it anonymously or pseudonymously, or, in the McPhersonian manner, attesting to the absolute authenticity of the work

11 One of the literary developments evolving from seventeenth century contemporary social trends was the publication of collected letters which led later to the epistolary novel. While the epistolae poeticae has been with us for a millenium and had served entertaining as well as didactic purposes throughout the centuries from the *Letters to the Corinthians* to Ovid's *Heroids* and *Heloise and Abelard*, it was the seventeenth century with its ever-increasing emphasis on letter writing in real life which heralded an era of immense epistolary production both fictional and authentic.

12 It must be kept in mind that many of the early novels were read aloud to family and friends and the first person narrative was most advantageous for such a practice for it established immediacy of the experience between narrator and audience, conveying at the same time an impression of authenticity.

they were about to "edit." *Robinson Crusoe* (1710) and *The Private Memoirs and Confession of a Justified Sinner* (1824) are outstanding examples of such artistic deceit. The lengths to which an author would occasionally go in order to dupe the public can best be judged from Hogg's effort. He not only included a facsimile page of the "original manuscript," but actually superimposed the confession (part two of the novel) upon the "factual data" obtained from the "family history" of both the protagonist and the antagonist. The composite work was then submitted to the reader's examination and evaluation by an anonymous "editor." Hogg's work, being a rather brilliantly arranged piece of fiction, is solid enough to stand on its artistic merits, and one cannot help but wonder today why an author would go to such lengths to keep up the pretense in order to deceive the public. One obvious answer, of course, is that the author tried to cater to public taste. Countless critics would immediately counter that such a statement can hardly stand closer scrutiny. Literary history and criticism demonstrate amply that it is the artist who shapes and influences public taste and not vice versa. But in this particular instance it seems the only plausible explanation. Producing a best-seller at the sacrifice of ethical and sometimes even aesthetic considerations, i.e., catering to public taste, may allow any author freedom and leisure to concentrate on a project near and dear to his heart which may not be marketable at all, or only in a very limited way.[13] Bowing to public taste thus becomes, in the light of self-preservation, a pardonable offense for the artist.

But what is it, we may ask, that compels us, the reader — regardless of our education or lack of it — to read any autobiographical

---

13 Herman Melville is certainly the rule rather than the exception when he writes: "I am so pulled hither and thither by circumstances. The calm, the coolness, the silent grass-growing mood in which a man OUGHT always to compose, — that, I fear, can seldom be mine. Dollars damn me; and the malicious devil is forever grinning in upon me, holding the door ajar. ... What I feel most moved to write, that is banned, — it will not pay. So the product is a final hash, and all my books are botches." (Letter to Nathanial Hawthorne, dated June 1851) quoted in *Novelists on the Novel*, ed. Miriam Allott, New York, Columbia University Press, 1959, p. 126.

utterings with such avidity? Is it mere curiosity? Is it edification we hope to find? Or could it be that we derive a not too small amount of smug satisfaction and self-assurance from the fact that others, just like ourselves, going through trial and errors, were subject to human weaknesses and shortcomings and acted at times ludicrously, pompously, and contemptibly. Malcolm Muggeridge, while ridiculing the mania for autobiographical writings, cannot help but admit to his own addiction to them:

> Autobiographies of contemporary worthies, however foolish, lying, pretentious, and banal they may be, never fail to hold the attention of readers like myself who are obsessively interested in the contemporary scene. Indeed, in a sense, the more foolish they are, the more enthralling. A Churchill with his rhetoric and cinerama technique soon palls, but a Clynes or Halifax or a John Simon, a Reith or a Hoare — these are delectable. The grease-paint competence of the one (to Gibbon what Napoleon III was to Buonaparte) is contrived, and therefore, in the end tiresome; the sheer artlessness of the others makes them an inexhaustible diversion.[14]

Bonamy Dobrée, too, ponders the question why we read autobiography with undiminished gusto:

> Well, curiosity, naturally; that love of gossip which is the cement of all societies, primitive or otherwise, which we dignify by calling it the desire to know about human nature ... We want to know somebody else intimately, gain contact with another human being, this in part being the object of all reading: we need to some extent to share the life of another creature such as we are.[15]

However, it is not only out of love for gossip that we turn to these writings. For many readers it is a deep-rooted yearning to understand the problems of another individual and his time, to see how he coped

---

14 Malcolm Muggeridge, "Lives of Great Men All Remind Us," *The New Statesman and Nation*, June 15, 1957, p. 771. It is somewhat amusing to see that Muggeridge, too, succumbed in the end to the temptation of writing his autobiography (*Chronicle of Wasted Time*, Morrow, 1944).
15 Bonamy Dobrée, "Some Literary Autobiographies of the Present Age," *Sewanee Review*, LXIV, Fall 1956, pp. 689-706. Dobrée, like Misch, includes indiscriminately any autobiographical writings of sorts (memoirs, letters, autobiographical novels, and episodes) in his discussion.

with them so that they may better understand themselves and their time. In such works they can trace man's ardent hopes and human weaknesses, his great aspirations and disillusions, his eternal strife to come to terms with the real and the ideal.

A recent publication by Dorothy Collet substantiates the notion that neither public avidity for autobiographical writings nor the attitudes of writers who would like to see their output, *coûte que coûte*, in print, has changed markedly during the past two-hundred and fifty years. Nor has the modern reader become more discriminate. Ms. Collet, confession writer and editor, points to the existence of an enormous and constant demand for the "properly structured, typical confession story" in this country. She advises the would-be "confession writer" that

> ... So many of the readers like to believe that the story was actually written by the narrator of that story. And for those who don't believe this, the illusion must be kept intact for the all-important tone of reality.[16]

From sheer volume alone it can be seen that autobiographical writings, just like poetry, drama, or the epic, have constituted throughout the centuries an important part of our literary tradition. At times almost extinct (from the fourth to the fourteenth century), they have at other times almost outnumbered other literary productions (for example the vast number of religious confessions during the seventeenth century). Yet, while the drama and the epic follow very distinct patterns and forms, i.e., a set of coherent principles, the author of an autobiography adheres to no set rules and accepts no external forms and limitations. Saint Augustine (345-430) wrote his *Confessions* in a beautifully limpid prose showing internal as well as external structure,[17] betraying the scholar of rhetoric and literature, but also the ecstatically happy man who has found temporal happiness and eternal salvation. Montaigne (1533-1592) composed

---

16 Dorothy Collet, *Writing of Modern Confession Story*, Boston, The Writer, Inc., 1951, p. 5.

17 cf. William C. Spengemann, "Augustine and Romantic Autobiography," an unpublished paper presented at the MLA December Meeting in New York, 1974.

his *Essays* in the diction of the philosopher, somewhat dry, often stylistically awkward, fascinating the reader forever anew with the multiplicity of his preoccupation, his intellectual aloofness, and his keen sense of humor. David Hume gives in his *Life* (published in 1777) a brief outline of his literary career and his belated popularity with the reading public, without neglecting to leave a picture of his own character. Jane Hoskens, whose *Life and Spiritual Sufferings* was published in 1771 in Philadelphia, is a representative of countless similar autobiographical writers discussing religious conversion, missionary work in foreign countries, her experiences as a school mistress, and her life in a big town (London). Some autobiographers preferred to look back upon their entire life and reminisce, others contented themselves with retracing experiences of childhood and early youth[18].

The autobiographers come from all walks of life. Their experiences vary from the most trite to the most sublime. Some have extensive literary backgrounds, others none whatsoever. As a consequence, the literary quality from the point of view of form and content varies considerably from work to work, or as Mr. Matthews points out: "the autobiography cannot pretend to be the most elegant of literary genres."[19] Yet, though greatly varied in form and content as these works are, all of these writers had one objective: they wanted to write the story of their lives. Each one felt that his life, in one way or another, had been an extraordinary life, worthy to be recorded and to be made public. And although none of these autobiographers worked within any formal guidelines (which are an absolute must for other genres), an unwritten creed formed the basis of their writings: they all wrote in retrospect, they told the experiences of their lives (whether as a shining example to be emulated or a damnable example to be avoided). They had no reason to falsify or to dis-

---

18 William Beloe published his autobiography, *Sexagenarian*, in 1817, combining scholarly reminiscences with accounts of social and personal affairs of his very active and interesting life, while Ann Taylor Gilbert, *Autobiography* (1784), discusses only her youth from 1782-1813 in Lavenham and Colchester.

19 William Matthews, *British Autobiographies* (An Annotated Bibliography of British Autobiographies Published or Written Before 1951), Berkeley and Los Angeles, University of California Press, 1955.

simulate their experience.[20] It is only after 1770, when poets and professional writers discovered the literary possibilities inherent in the usually lackluster autobiography that new objectives instituted considerable and far reaching changes within the genre.

While comprehensive studies about the autobiographical genre are sorely lacking, several smaller but valuable comparative studies have recently emerged, treating either one or more elements common to a given number of autobiographies, or showing common denominators in the work of two or more authors.[21] The major flaw of these studies is, ironically enough, the lack of a satisfying definition of the form itself. For Professor Misch, who, in the course of almost sixty years, has given us the most comprehensive compilation of autobiographical writings, autobiography comprises all writings which include any autobiographical data.[22] Consequently he includes in his collection inscriptions on Egyptian tombs (provided they were written by the occupants themselves, prior to their demise), poems, letters, and other lyrical and prose writings. Misch's sole criterion is that these writings relate to the personal experiences and/or feelings of the author.[23]

20 For a substantial list of such autobiographies cf. William Matthews, *op. cit.*; Marianne Beyer-Fröhlich, *Deutsche Selbstzeugnisse*, 10 Volumes, Leipzig, Verlag Philipp Reclam jun., 1933; and Philippe Lejeune, *L'Autobiographie en France*, Paris, Librairie Armand Colin, 1971.

21 See John N. Morris, *Version of the Self*, New York, Basic Books, 1966. Roy Pascal, *Design and Truth in Autobiography*, Cambridge, Mass., Harvard University Press, 1960. Philippe Lejeune op. cit.

22 Georg Misch, *Geschichte der Autobiographie*, 4 Vol. 8 parts, Frankfurt/Main, G. Schulte-Bulmke Verlag, 1969.

23 The lack of a clear definition is not only painfully apparent in the domain of autobiographical writings, but it seems to plague the very concept of literature itself. "The confusion," writes Mary Colum, "that exists at present between literature and all sorts of writing is partly due to the uncritical manner in which literary history has been written, in which pure literature is considered in the same volume, and even in the same chapter, with historical works, with political works, which sometimes are literature and sometimes only information, or sometimes mere opinions, and with works of science, which are almost never literature, with oratory and pamphleteering, which commonly are forms outside of literature." *From These Roots, The Ideas That Have Made Modern Literature*, New York, N.Y., Scribners, 1938.

22

Morris tells us that autobiography is "a species of historical narrative of events occurring in time" and considers its simplest form a "straightforward chronicle." Pascal, on the other hand, is much more selective. He differentiates autobiography from diary, chronicle, memoirs, and letters. "Autobiography," he says, "involves a distinctive attitude on the part of the author, a distinctive mode of presentation — and, if one is concerned with its historical significance, gives evidence of a distinctive psychological characteristic of European civilization."[24] It is a review of life from a particular moment in time and must be systematically retrospective. Pascal definitely attributes "genre" status to the autobiography, for he directs his examinations at "this genre as it has become established and recognized."[25]

Generally the classification of a work according to its literary genre presents no problems, especially since the original Aristotelian and Horatian categories have in the course of the centuries been broken down considerably into subgenres and subspecies in order to accommodate virtually the entire literary production. But while these subdivisions facilitate categorization, they impose at the same time certain limitations. Each work assigned to a given genre must share the basic characteristics of all the other works within this genre.[26] René Wellek assigns those works to a given literary genre whose "inner form (attitude, tone, purpose — more crudely subject and audience)" coincides with the "outer form (specific meter and structure)." Yet, though we have come a long way since the postulation of the original genres, and though many subgenres have evolved (and in all probability will continue to evolve) and have been acknowledged by literary critics, one or the other literary form seems to resist any attempt of classification.[27] Confessions, *Selbstbekennt-*

---

24 Roy Pascal, *op. cit.*, p. 9.
25 René Wellek, by contrast, categorically refuses autobiography a place in the field of literature and relegates it to "other writings." (*Theory of Literature*, New York, Harcourt, Brace and Co., 1942).
26 cf. Ferdinand Brunetière, *L'Evolution des genres litéraires*, Paris: Colin, 1948.
27 W. V. Ruttkowski, — *Die Literarischen Gattungen*, Bern, A. Francke A.G. Verlag, 1968. The existence of the different genres is generally acknowledged

nisse, and autobiographies, which by their very nature must be unique and highly individualistic, seem to fall into this category. And it is writers like Rousseau, Wordsworth, and De Quincey who, rather than contributing to the solidification of the genre, signal the beginning of the gradual erosion of its "inner" as well as its "outer form." It is therefore not surprising that authors and critics dealing with these writings are for the most part reluctant to attach any label or to attempt any classification. Even Misch is exceedingly careful and sometimes downright vague when it comes to any sort of definition.

> The autobiography is a literary genre unlike any other. Its limits are more fluid and cannot be fixed from without and determined according to form as it can be done with lyrics, epics, and drama, which — once their "primal phenomenon" has emerged from the dark depths of undivided potentiality — are developed according to a unified form despite all the temporal, national, and individual multiplicity of the creations.[28]

Basically, this tells us absolutely nothing as far as any common characteristics are concerned, except that autobiography is not to be considered a genre in the traditional sense. And Misch continues:

> Considered in their entity autobiographical writings show indeed, a protean character. This literary genre shirks a definition more obstinately than the most common forms of literature. A definition can hardly come closer than an explanation of the term itself: the description (graphia) of a life (bio) of an individual by himself. (auto)[29]

> though feeling as to their validity and usefulness varies greatly. From time to time vehement polemics such as the one between V. Valentic and Th. Lipps arise (*Zeitschrift für vergleichende Literaturwissenschaft,* Neue Folge, Bd. 5, Berlin, 1892) B. Croce, for example, insists on the uniqueness of each literary work, which therefore defies any classification.

28 Georg Misch, *op. cit.,* p. 6.
29 The etymology of the word "autobiography" is of some interest. The first mention of it was made, according to the OED, by Robert Southey in 1809 in a review of Portuguese literature. Prior to that date all such writings appeared as confessions, memoirs, cahiers, life story, *Selbsterlebnis, Lebenserinnerungen,* etc. In other words, works written prior to that date (i.e., Cellini's *Autobiography*), acquired their titles with the help of a well-meaning editor at a much later date, sometime during the nineteenth or twentieth century.

Yet "genre" (Literaturgattung) it is! Can and will the literary critic and historian be satisfied with such an all-inclusive definition or would the acceptance of it wreak havoc with other, solidly established genres? Would not such a definition necessitate a sub-division: poetry-autobiographical poetry, letters-autobiographical letters, novel-autobiographical novel? The possibilities are unlimited. Since each of the genres and subgenres already must have a certain amount of elasticity to compensate for individual differences, would such an undertaking not destroy whatever little cohesion exists within the genres? For Misch tells us:

> No form is foreign to it [the autobiography]. Prayer, monologue, factual account, invented court speech or rhetorical declamation, scientifically or artistically descriptive characteristic, lyric and confession, letter and literary portraits, family chronicle and courtly memoirs, historical accounts of pure subject matter, pragmatic and developmental history or fiction, the novel and the biography within their different categories, the epic, even the drama-autobiography appeared within all these forms.[30]

It is primarily due to the nature of such a definition (or lack of it) that Professor Misch's work attained its vast proportions, even though he included little of the nineteenth and nothing of the prolific autobiographic production of the twentieth century. The epitaph figures in it, along with letters, essays, and any other literary forms. To accept such a definition (and therefore the multiplicity of works which comply with it) would frustrate beforehand any attempt to discover common elements and characteristics which would make it feasible to group certain writings as belonging to the "genre" of autobiography.

If Misch's definition is an experience in frustration, we rarely fare any better with other critics. E.S. Bates tells us that the common denominator of autobiographies is their preoccupation "with what is of fundamental significance as regards self-revealed personality, after thorough consideration." He considers the factor of "reconsideration" as the "distinctive characteristic of autobiography." And add-

---

30 Georg Misch, *op. cit.*, p. 15, brackets are mine.

ing to our confusion and frustration, he tells us that "autobiography, in fact, is not so much a species of literature as an idea."[31]

Since Bates attributes no importance to spatial and/or temporal elements, nor to the psychological modifications that these "reconsiderations" could (and invariably do) work, his definition is also too vague. Again, it would include at least half of the entire literary production, whether a short poem, an essay, or a lengthy novel, wherever and whenever the narrator or persona reveals personal experiences and observations on his life and the world in general. All of these could represent precisely such "reconsiderations" of the author. Such a definition would include such writings as Nobel's *Life*, which may qualify as an epitaph of questionable taste, but surely not as an autobiography.[32] Since Professor Bates' clearly stated intent is "to establish that autobiography and its uses constitute a source of knowledge that is unfamiliar and to endeavour to render both of them less unfamiliar and more intelligible and to facilitate further inquiry" we should not censure him too severely for providing a basically harmless definition which, however, upon closer examination, becomes almost meaningless.

A fairly recent and very good, and above all, very courageous study is John N. Morris' *Version of the Self.* Yet again, when it comes to making a commitment to definition, he too, is most reluctant to do so.

> All that is required of the autobiographer — it is a very large "all" — is that his language and his design answer to the truth of his experience — but he must convince us that his book is living up to living his life.[33]

---

31 E.S. Bates, *Inside Out — Introduction to Autobiography*, New York, Sheridon House, 1937, p. 2.

32 "Alfred Nobel — his miserable existence should have been terminated at birth by a humane doctor as he drew his first howling breath. Principal virtues: keeping his nails clean and never being a burden to anyone. Principal faults: that he has no family, is bad-tempered and has a poor digestion. One and only wish: not to be buried alive. Greatest sin: that he does not worship Mammon. Important events in his life: none." quoted by E.S. Bates, *op. cit.*

33 John N. Morris, *op. cit.*

Here the key word is the "truth of his experience." Much has been written about "truth" in autobiography. Historical facts, personal letters, and accounts of contemporaries have been compared with a given autobiography in order to establish its factual veracity. But is it this kind of "truth" that Morris is concerned with? It could not be, for who is to judge what is truth and what glorified recollection? H.G. Wells hits upon the crux of the matter when he says:

> A man, who tries to behave as he conceives he should behave, may be satisfactorily honest in restraining, ignoring, and disavowing many of his innate motives and dispositions. The mask, the persona, of the Happy Hypocrite became at last his true face.[34]

This statement becomes especially meaningful when we later examine Rousseau's *Confessions*. And there is a good grain of truth in Wells' statement that all men are imperfect saints and heroes, as well as liars. Who is to say that Jean-Jacques Rousseau did not believe every single detail of his *Confessions* to be nothing but the naked truth? In the painful process of soul-searching, circumstances and events may have taken on dimensions which to him were true and authentic, while to some of his most scrupulous critics they seemed distorted and/or deliberately falsified. The omission of one incident or the addition of another may alter the slant of presentation. We all are aware of the capricious tricks time seems to play on our memories when events, important at the time of their occurrence, slowly fade out of our life to be replaced by what seemed previously insignificant details, which now, in retrospect, seem more influential upon our development and therefore take on greater dimensions. Depending on the mental makeup of a given person and his success or adversities in life, the dominating tone of his writing will be either positive or negative, the pleasant or the sinister will be predominant. An old cantankerous fellow like Grillparzer will think mostly of his misfortunes and mishaps to demonstrate the "truth of his experience," while his happy-go-lucky brother may recollect mostly pleasant events in his life. The very same incident seen by five different

---

34 H.G. Wells, *Experiment in Autobiography*, New York, The Macmillan Company, 1934, p. 10.

people, may yield five entirely different accounts, each of which is, according to its author, "true to the experience." (Every police inspector, forever frustrated in his work by such different accounts, can testify to this commonplace occurrence.) So it seems that Morris touches at the heart of a valid definition with his demand for "truth of experience" and the necessity to convince us "that his [the autobiographer's] book is *living up to living* his life." If we add to this basic requirement that the work must have been written in retrospect, that it must cover a substantial number of years, and that it must give testimony of how a given event or experience over a period of years influenced or perhaps modified that author's outlook on or attitude toward life, then we have, regardless of its title, a valid definition of the subject matter of the conventional autobiography as it was written up to ca. 1770. Although it is the aspect of writing in retrospect which accounts for numerous anachronisms (which seem to increase in direct relation to the length of the time period the author tries to cover), yet this is probably the second most important aspect of a good conventional autobiography. If we omit it, we have a journal or diary, or even letters. Though each of these reveals a great deal about the author, neither shows a continuous spiritual or intellectual development in relation to external stimuli.[35] Such a definition would rule out writings such as Nobel's *Life*, for we there perceive not a man living his life, but rather a lump of matter, untouched by human life forces and registering purely physical changes: birth, youth, middle age, old age, without any interrelation whatsoever, without the slightest sign of spiritual and mental growth or even any awareness of these purely human properties. It also rules out both the autobiographical novel (which in our days has become increasingly popular), as well as the fictional autobiography or confession.

35 Even as renowned a letter writer as Mme. de Sevigné presents a very one-sided portraiture. The same is true about the memoir, which is much too much concerned with external events and usually neglects the spiritual and/or intellectual changes that these events bring about in the author. The memoir has long been the favorite form of expression of politicians, officers, and courtiers. (The memoir, incidentally, appeals to a much more limited range of readers than the autobiography.)

I have deliberately dwelt on the problem of definition rather lengthily at the risk of appearing tedious, because I feel it is at the bottom of much confusion surrounding autobiographical writings. The lack of a clear definition, the vagueness which pervades many worthwhile newer studies, leads to ever-increasing confusion instead of elucidation, so that the student finds such works as *War and Peace, Madame Bovary,* or *Remembrance of Things Past* treated as autobiographies.[36] A clear definition is all the more important when the reader can neither rely on the title of the work, nor on the opening statement of the author's intent, as we shall see below.

My definition, a sincere recording in retrospect of a lifetime (or at least a considerable number of years) of experiences, actions, and interactions and their immediate and long range effects upon the individual, seems to accommodate such diverse writings as Saint Augustine's *Confessions,* Cellini's *Autobiography*, Montaigne's *Essays*, and thousands more of lesser renown, published before 1770. But reading James Hogg's *Confessions of a Justified Sinner* or, to cite a more modern example, Proust's *Remembrance of Things Past*, we realize that we are no longer dealing with the autobiography as the living testimony of a man's life, but rather with a literary work, where the author uses all the conventions of the established autobiography to produce a work of fiction. The opening lines of radically different works often bear a striking resemblance:

1. As I take up my pen at leisure and in complete retirement − in good health, furthermore, though tired, so tired that I shall only be able to proceed by short stages and with frequent pauses for rest − as I take up my pen, then, to commit my confessions to the patient paper in my own neat and attractive handwriting, I am assailed by a brief misgiving about the educational background I bring to an intellectual enterprise of this kind. But since everything I have to record derives from my own immediate experience, errors, and passions, and since I am therefore in complete command of my material, the doubt can apply only to my own tact and propriety of expression, and in my own view these are less the product of study than of natural talent and a good home environment.[37]

36 See, for example, Esther Salaman, *The Great Confession*, London, Allen Lane-The Penguin Press, 1973.

37 Thomas Mann, *Confessions of Felix Krull, Confidence Man*, tr. Denver Lindley, New York, The New American Library Inc., 1963.

2. All men of what-soever quality they be, who have done anything of excellence, ought, if they are persons of truth and honesty, to describe their life with their own hand; but they ought not attempt so fine an enterprise till they have passed the age of forty. This duty occurs to my own mind now that I am travelling beyond the term of fifty-eight years, and am in Florence, the city of my birth. Many untoward things can I remember, such as happen to all who live upon our earth; and from those adversities I am now more free than at any previous period of my career.[38]

3. My life has been of trouble and turmoil; of change and vicissitude; of anger and exultation; of sorrow and of vengeance and my vengeance has been wreaked on its adversaries. Therefore, in the might of heaven I will sit down and write: I will let the wicked of this world know what I have done in faith of the promises, and justification by grace, that they may read and tremble, and bless their gods of silver and gold, that the minister of heaven was removed from the sphere before their blood was mingled with their sacrifices.

   I was born an outcast in the world, in which I was destined to act so conspicuous a part ...[39]

4. I am taking upon myself an endeavour which has no example and whose execution will have no imitators. I want to show to my fellow men a human being within the utmost truth of nature; and this human being shall be I.[40]

5. I here present you, courteous reader, with the record of a remarkable period of my life: and according to my application of it, I trust that it will prove not merely an interesting record, but, in a considerable degree, instructive.[41]

Thousands of similar opening lines could be quoted. Each of the given excerpts implies by its title as well as its content that we are

38 Benvenuto Cellini, *Autobiography*, tr. J. Addington Symonds, Roslyn, N.Y., Black's Readers Service Co., 1972.
39 James Hogg, *Private Memoirs and Confessions of a Justified Sinner*, Part III, London, Oxford University Press, 1969.
40 Jean Jacques Rousseau, *Les Confessions*, Paris, Librairie Générale Française, Edition de la Pleiade, 1963.
41 Thomas De Quincey, *Confessions of An English Opium-Eater*, London, Macdonald and Co., Ltd., 1956.

dealing with a genuine autobiography — (four are entitled *Confession*, the fifth *Autobiography*). Yet only one of the works, excerpt two, is a truly conventional autobiography. Excerpts four and, to an even greater extent, five constitute a marked deviation from the established norm, and the other two works are strictly fiction. Considering that Philippe LeJeune relied heavily on such passages as the ones quoted above (he calls them "le pacte autobiographique" between the reader and the writer) in determining whether a work be conventional and therefore true autobiography or merely fiction, we can see how terribly misleading such opening statements can be. LeJeune omitted all "seemingly autobiographical writings" from his bibliography if such a statement was lacking. He does, however, cautiously point to the inconclusiveness of such statements and recommends prior readings of critical studies and the author's biography in order to be able to verify the authenticity of any given "autobiography." Barret Mandel is more specific when he differentiates between an autobiographer and a writer of fiction:

> The autobiographer may never falsify his facts for a fictional purpose without giving up his claim to the name of autobiographer.[42]

Although the passing off of fake or fictional autobiography for the real thing (the conventional autobiography) is generally accepted as a longstanding literary convention, it is — to say the least — confusing and annoying to the reader in general but especially to the literary critic who is compelled to spend a considerable amount of time playing detective before he can even attempt looking at the work itself. Yet, while the counterfeiter would be put behind bars, and the copying and imitating painters be castigated, there is absolutely no stigma attached to such practice by the writer. In order to understand this phenomenon it is necessary to glance back at the literary activities of the eighteenth century.

The greatest single contribution to literature of the eighteenth century was the novel.[43] The popularity of this new genre can best

42 B.J. Mandel, "The Autobiographer's Art," *Journal of Aesthetics and Art Criticism*, XXVI, December 1968, pp. 215-216.

43 "If by the term 'novel' we mean simply prose fiction of some length this literary form has a long history indeed. But if we define it with some rigor

be seen by the rapid increase in publication figures.[44] The reading public in Germany and England alone is estimated to have increased twelve to fourteen times during the eighteenth century. Obviously the novel was not born over night, rather, it made and is still making extensive use of already existing literary forms, themes, and conventions.[45] Prior to the wide-spread acceptance of the novel, the letter, both personal and fictional, had been one of the most popular literary forms of the eighteenth century. Neither the letter nor the novelistic prose writings were entirely new. Their original concept can, with some persistence, be traced back to antiquity.[46] The form

in terms of a regular structure of plot, then the novel begins as a serious genre in mid-eighteenth century England. Its development at this time owes more to the novels of Fielding, than those of any other writer. Moreover, the Preface to Joseph Andrews (1742) and the introductory chapters to the various books of *Tom Jones* are the first serious criticism of the novel that we have." W.J. Bates, *Criticism: Major Texts*, New York, Harcourt, Brace and Co., 1952.

44 According to Wolfgang J. Kayser around 1740 annually 10 novels appeared; around 1770 there were one hundred; by the year 1785 there were already three hundred novels being published, and around 1800 about five hundred annually. In the twentieth century two thousand novels are annually being published in Germany. He gives the same figures for England. cf. Wolfgang Kayser, *Die Entstehung des modernen Romans*, 4. Auflage, Stuttgart, J.B. Metzlersche Verlagsfachhandlung, 1963.

45 See David Daiches, *A Critical History of English Literature*, 2nd edition, vol. 2, London, Secker and Warburg, 1960.

46 The tremendous popularity of the epistolary novel sharply declined after the 1820's as other forms of the novel gained in popularity. According to Jost, publication figures show a total of 1000 epistolary novels between 1740 and 1820 of which roughly twenty were masterpieces, fifty became classics, and about three hundred retain historical interest. See François Jost, "Le roman épistolaire et la technique narrative au XVIII siècle," *Comparative Literature Studies*, III, 1966, pp. 397-427.

Daniel Mornet, researching the extent of perusal of the epistolary novel, shows that such writings were tremendously popular in eighteenth century France, that, in fact, one third of all books in 392 Parisian libraries between 1740 and 1760 consisted of epistolary novels. See Daniel Mornet, "Les enseignements des bibliothèques privées," *Revue D'Histoire Littéraire de la France*, XVII, 1910, pp. 449-496.

of the personal letter, whose usage — as we have seen before — had been tremendously growing in popularity already in the seventeenth century, was first used as a basis for collections of fictional letters. The personal experience, related in an intimate, confidential manner was used more and more frequently as the subject matter for fictional works. The charm of the personal letter is based on its intimacy, the very personal feelings and emotions it conveys. It postulates a close, friendly person-to-person relationship between reader and writer and thus guarantees an emotional response by its very immediacy. The epistolary novel is a direct off-spring of the collected letters, and the best of these novels (Richardson's *Clarissa Harlowe*, Rousseau's *Nouvelle Heloise*, Goethe's *The Sorrows of Young Werther*) retain this immediacy by opening, so-to-speak, a side-window to let the reader take part in the intimate lives of the letter writers.

Another exceedingly popular literary form of the century, also thoroughly exploited by novelists, was the *Tatsachenbericht*, the factual account or travelogue. Extensive travel, adventure, vivid interest in scientific expeditions and discoveries supplied ample raw material for the novelist. Again, in their original form these were first-person accounts and narratives by an author who had witnessed the strangest events, survived the most trying ordeals of raging seas, strange lands, and strange, exotic people. The strangest and most incongruous events received the seal of verisimilitude, because the narrator had been there, had witnessed them. Since in many cases these eyewitness-accounts of exotic ventures often surpassed the wildest feats of the imagination, their adaptation and transformation into the realm of fiction presented no problem for the novelists. Churning out novel after novel in rapid succession to satisfy public demands, they must have most eagerly turned to these accounts for new and exciting subject matter which would sufficiently interest and entertain the readers without exerting too much strain on the writer's imaginative faculty. By basing their novels on such accounts, they complied at the same time with Fielding's formula for the novel: "The great art of all poetry is to mix truth with fiction, in order to join the credible with the surprising.[47] In this manner the

47 Henry Fielding, *The History of Tom Jones, A Foundling* (1749) quoted in

novel established itself on the literary scene in a record time and with record publication figures. Such growth, however, was only possible because the novelist used and poetically transformed other already well established and well developed literary forms. He had used the letter and the *Tatsachenbericht* for this end and it was only a matter of time, before one writer was to transform the autobiography to comply with his particular aim and objective.

The novel is one art form which achieved great popularity and ready acceptance because of its widespread appeal to the European middle class. This appeal was not based on aesthetic considerations or artistic appreciation, but rather on the individual author's ability to "colour, decorate, and embellish his novels, as most agreeably to flatter" the reader's "humour, and most highly promise to entertain, captivate and enchant his mind."[48] The new reader was often an indiscriminate reader all too frequently accommodated by the indiscriminate writer, the amateur. The traditionally oriented elite of writers adhered to poetry, treating the newly emerging novel, if not with outright contempt, at least with aloofness.[49] These early novelists on the other hand, displayed a keen sense of business. They were not yet plagued by the characteristic arrogance of the adherents of the later *art pour l'art* movement and their successors who proclaimed to be writing exclusively for their own gratification and enjoyment. The eighteenth century reader wanted to be entertained and enchanted. The writers obliged. The demand for the "true life story," for verisimilitude, *Wahrscheinlichkeit*, and *vraisemblence*

Novelists on the Novel, edit. Miriam Allott, New York, Columbia University Press, 1959, p. 61.

48 Sarah Fielding, *Introduction to the Lives of Cleopatra and Octavia*, (1757) quoted in *Novelists on the Novel, op. cit.*, p. 44.

49 "Au cours du XVIIIe siècle, le roman cherche ses techniques et ses méthodes; tant qu'il n'aura point trouvé sa forme, il restera un genre méconnu et méprisé. En 1780 encore, Johann Karl Wenzel, dans la preface de son *Hermann und Ulricke*, doit constater ce fait: "Der Roman ist eine Dichtungsart, die am meisten verachtet und am meisten gelesen wird." 1784 Laclos (dans une critique de *Cecilia*, roman de Fanny Burney); "De tous genres d'ouvrages qui produit la littérature, il en est peu moins estimés qui celui des romans; mais il n'y en a aucun de plus généralement et de plus avidement lu." F. Jost, *op. cit.*, p. 397.

became the motto of the day: The novelist obligingly supplied the first person novel, equipped with an appropriate preface explaining how the present author was merely editing an account entrusted to him by such and such a person, a dying friend, or found by chance in a secret closet in such and such a remote manor or farmhouse.[50] Defoe was one of the earliest novelists to practice this deceit extensively. Hogg, a century later, still perpetuated it. Countless others applied in greater or lesser degree the same technique, passing off a work of fiction for a true life story. Clara Reeve probably summed up best what was expected of the novel by her contemporaries:

> The novel gives a familiar relation of such things, as pass every day before our eyes, such as may happen to our friend, to ourselves; and the perfection of it is to represent every scene in so easy and natural a manner, and to make them appear so probable, as to deceive us into a persuasion (at least while we are reading) that all is real, until we are affected by the joys or distresses of the persons in the story, as if they were our own.[51]

There is a striking similarity between these words and those quoted on page 20 by Dorothy Collet. They both show just how little the demands of the reading masses have changed in the course of the centuries.

By 1785 the epistolary, the picaresque, the gothic, the historic, and the adventure novel, with or without an explaining, admonishing, justifying, or edifying narrator, had become popularized. The *Ich-Roman* (or first-person novel), in almost any case a strictly fictional account, figured prominently among all of these. But if the middle of the eighteenth century had been a period of "transition

---

50 "Le croyable a de tout temps constitué la matière littéraire, et tout l'art de l'écrivain consiste à faire accepter — fort provisoirement, parfois — l'irréel comme réel le fictif comme vrai." ... Tout, dans la technique même que l'on choisit, doit corroborer, chez le lecteur, l'impression d'un recit susceptible de verification. On exhume et exhibe des parchemins, toujours l'auteur produit ou fait semblant de produire ses preuves. F. Jost, *op. cit.*, pp. 339-397.

51 Clara Reeve, *The Progress of Romance* (1785) quoted in *Novelists on the Novel, op. cit.*, p. 47.

and experiment in poetic style and subjects"[52] the last part of the century ushered in a new ideology, a new concept of man's individuality and greatness which was to find expression through the Romantic poets and writers. It was to add new dimensions to aestheticism and to affect every existing literary form, including the autobiography. It was the combination of these two elements, the still evolving and developing novel and some of the basic concepts underlying Romanticism which brought about the most decisive changes within the autobiographical genre. On the one hand, we see the novelist obeying the dictates of public demand, encroaching upon this well-established literary form in his search for new subject matter; on the other hand new concepts in literary theory and creativity are compelling poet and writer to search relentlessly both for greater and more complete consciousness and the means to express it. And the autobiography offers itself as the ideal means for such an end.

It is somewhat simplistic to consider the autobiography — as J. Cox has done, the "phenomenon," i.e., the direct outgrowth of the American and the French Revolutions, simply because a great number of autobiographies emerged in their wake.[53] One of the greatest, if not the greatest autobiography of all times, Jean-Jacques Rousseau's *Confessions*, had been written from 1766-1770 and published posthumously in 1782, more than seven years before the French Revolution. Preoccupation with autobiographies and therefore with one's self should rather be considered as a manifestation of new trends, thoughts, and drives within an increasingly more urbanized and industrialized society:

52 David Daiches, *op. cit.*, p. 856.
53 Cox, pointing to such writings as Franklin's, Henry Adams', and Thoreau's and an equally prominent number of French autobiographical works, assures his readers that England — outside the realms of the liberating and energy-releasing throngs of revolution — concentrated on the writing of LIVES (*Boswell's Life of Johnson*). He maintains complete silence in regard to the works of Wordsworth, De Quincey, Coleridge, et al. "With Franklin," he tells us, "came consciousness, total consciousness in the form of autobiography — a history of a self-made life, written by the man who made it." James Cox, "Autobiography and America" in *Aspects of the Narrative*, ed. J.H. Miller, New York and London, Columbia University Press, 1971.

In pre-Romantic imagery the world of social and civilized life, however evil or corrupt, and however thoroughly denounced was still the gateway to identity: man for pre-Romantic poets was still primarily a social and civilized being and could not progress except through his social heritage. In a great deal of romantic imagery human society is thought of as leading to alienation rather than identity and this sense increases steadily throughout the nineteenth century as literature becomes more and more ironic in both tone and structure. In Romanticism there is an emphasis on the false identity of the conforming group, even for the most conservative Romantics the real social values are in a tradition which has probably been lost anyway and, by contrast, on a kind of creative and healing alienation to be gained from a solitary contact with the order of nature outside society.[54]

In an effort to regain "man's original state"--i.e., his lost innocence and greater consciousness—writers started to focus their attention on their innermost thoughts and emotions. Rousseau in France, Herder, Novalis, Wackenroder in Germany, Blake, Wordsworth, De Quincey in England, pursued much the same goal. If Everett Knight is correct in saying that it is in the novel that our *culture* has most consistently and profoundly examined itself,[55] then we can expand this statement and say that it is in the autobiography that *man* has most consistently and profoundly examined himself. In direct proportion in which the feeling of disillusionment with and alienation from society increases, the writing of autobiography catches momentum and gains in importance.

If the calculated withdrawal or alienation from society and the masses gave rise to probing self-analysis and introspection and led to the writing of a substantial number of autobiographies, it also heralded a new concept of art and the artist. Aesthetic discussions concerning beauty abounded during the eighteenth century and reached their culmination around 1800. Beauty, natural beauty, was to be an important element in the new *Menschheitsideal*, an important ingredient of the formula for happiness. Walter Killy's

54 Northrop Frye, *A Study of English Romanticism*, New York, Random House, 1968, p. 46.
55 Everett Knight, *A Theory of the Classical Novel*, London, Routledge and Kegan Paul, 1969.

remarks, aimed at literature in general, are of particular interest to our discussion of the evolution of the autobiography.

> A new reality, related and friendly to the art and beauty replaces, surpasses, and orders the empirical reality which the poet has assimilated not in order to destroy it, but to transmute it into his artistic whole.[56]

These remarks summarize exactly what happened to the conventional autobiography in Wordsworth's, De Quincey's as well as in Goethe's case. We could add Chateaubriand, Constant, George Sand, and hundreds of others. Personal experience, subjected to artistic demands, is turned into a literary creation and, though basically and fundmentally of an autobiographical nature, loses its claim to the conventional autobiography, for the author has--in the interest of *artistic* considerations–changed or modified the true nature of events and experiences.

Satisfying both the popular demand and the artist's inclination, the autobiographical novel represents a related literary development of this time. It flourished almost over night. Goethe (*The Sorrows of Young Werther*), Wackenroder (*Joseph Berglinger*), Schlegel (*Lucinde*), von Hardenberg (Novalis--*Heinrich von Ofterdingen*), and others cultivated it in Germany; Rousseau (La *nouvelle Heloïse*), Chateaubriand (*René*), Musset (*La Confession d'un enfant du siècle*), Stendhal (*La chartreuse de Parme*), among others in France.[57] The hero in each of these works shows unmistakable similarities to the author and the action often centers around one particular autobiographical event in the author's life. Scholars, for example, have spilled gallons of ink trying to establish (what is so apparent in *Dichtung und Wahrheit*) that young Werther's adventures could be traced to and compared with young Goethe's experiences in Sesenheim, that René's *ennui* and *mal de siècle* characterized Chateau-

---

56 Walter Killy, *Wirklichkeit und Kunstcharakter*, München, G.H. Beck'sche Verlagsbuchhandlung, 1963, p. 15.

57 Musset's *Confessions* and Stendhal's *Henri Brulard* are closer to Wordsworth's and Goethe's conception of the autobiography than to the autobiographical novel.

briand's state of mind as a young man, that Joseph Berglinger's travels and aesthetic experiences in the field of music and painting bore striking resemblance to Wackenroder's own education and experiences. Again, the fact that the author uses a personal experience or a state of mind as a point of departure or even as a central theme for his novel, does not make it an autobiography. Hazlitt's *Liber Amoris*, for example, is not an autobiography. The author elaborates on one single experience in his life, viz. the infatuation with his landlady's fickle daughter, while an autobiography must record such events and experiences over a substantial number of years. In many autobiographical novels the author does not attempt to describe a substantial part of his life, but rather concentrates on one segment. He does not record the events in a "truthful" and factual manner; rather he artistically transforms them to serve and further the aim of his envisioned work of art. And above all, he does not claim to be writing his autobiography, neither explicitly nor implicitly.

Looking at some of the most outstanding writers and the greatest masterpieces of our time, we find that the techniques (form, style, and subject matter treatment) of the autobiographical novel (which, it must be remembered, is first of all a novel and only incidentally and in some aspects autobiographical) have been refined and perfected. Such works, conceived and built on personal experience and/or emotions rather than born of the writer's imagination and fancy, are devoid of artifice and therefore portray the struggles and joys of the human condition more faithfully and more convincingly. David Perkins concludes that our contemporary poetry finds its main source in the great romantic writers.

> They [the romantic poets] found in themselves certain urgent notions, impressions, and ways of feeling which had not previously been exploited in poetry, and hence they had to create some relatively new technical means to represent the poet in the image of the discoverer, a man isolated in some difficult exploration or quest. It is a figure which aroused a mingled feeling of anxiety and pride, and it is one which has a certain historical justice. They were explorers and pioneers, and they have been followed by settlers and squatters who have both carried further and domesticated their discoveries. Periods of intense intellectual exploration are often followed by years of codification and cataloguing, when the new "points

and resting places in reasoning," as Keats called them, are pursued, refined, fitted together, and organized into a system. From one point of view, this process of refining describes what has been taking place in the literary history of the modern world. We are still living in the comet's tail of the nineteenth century.[58]

Much of Perkin's remarks is applicable not only for the romantic poets, but also for the romantic novelists. If I disagree with him, it is strictly a matter of semantics. The comet's tail is less luminous than its head. Yet such works as Rilke's *Notebooks of Malte Laurids Brigge*, Mann's *Tonio Kröger* or *The Buddenbrooks*, Gide's *The Immoralist*, Proust's *Remembrance of Things Past*, Joyce's *Portrait of the Artist*, or Tolstoy's *War and Peace* have achieved star-status in the literary skies every bit as luminous as their Romantic predecessors. But each one of these works has its origin in the romantic movement of the 1800's. Today the autobiographical novel seems to enjoy an ever-increasing popularity with both the writers themselves and the reading public. In fact, the modern writer seems to give preference to this kind of novel over the artistic autobiography of a Wordsworth or Goethe, for it allows his creative genius greater freedom because it imposes fewer restrictions. While the practice of publishing fictional autobiography as an authentic one (as in Hogg's case) has --on the whole--fallen in disuse, the writing of fictional autobiographies is still flourishing (cf. Thomas Mann: *Felix Krull, The Confessions of a Confidence Man* or Styron's *Confessions of Nat Turner*), and the writing of conventional autobiography has reached unprecedented heights in our modern age where introspection and psychoanalysis have become the rage.

---

58 David Perkins, *The Quest for Performanence*, Cambridge, Mass., Harvard University Press, 1959, pp. 2-3 –Brackets are mine.

CHAPTER II

JEAN-JACQUES ROUSSEAU (1712-1778)

Jean-Jacques Rousseau is generally looked upon as one of the fathers of modern man. He is, according to André Maurois, one of the few writers of whom it can be said: "but for him the whole of French literature would have taken a different direction."[1] This is particularly true in regard to the development of the autobiography. Not only did this writer give "country freshness" to French literature and a "taste of intimate and domestic sensibility," but he provided in his autobiography the first example of a *complete* "sincere" and often painful self-analysis. In his work we find a frank avowal of often contemptible "moral lapses," and with unprecedented candor, he speaks of the specific nature of his sensuality. "The taste for the cult of sincerity did not come naturally to men before Rousseau's days. . . . Not until Rousseau came upon the scene, do we find the writer who took pride in telling all."[2] Since this writer also introduced a new objective, i.e., he no longer was writing an autobiography for the sake of recording his life, his *Confessions* must form the logical *point d'appui* for my discussion of the evolution of the autobiographical genre.

The author himself points in his work repeatedly to the "uniqueness" of his life and the circumstances surrounding it. He feels that his emotions and feelings as well as his personal calamities are unique (i.e., they manifest themselves almost exclusively in the superlative). "I alone" is one of the most frequently resounding expressions throughout the work. He considers himself the most unhappy, the most misunderstood, the most misinterpreted, the most

---

1   André Maurois, *The Art of Writing*, London, The Bodley Head, 1960, p. 51.
2   Ibid, p. 53.

hated, but also the most sincere, the most loving, the most under-standing of all mortals. But the author is not only conscious of his extraordinary self, he is just as emphatic about the uniqueness of his *Confessions*.

Fully aware of the "uniqueness" of his rebellious attitude and mode of thought, of the frequently criticized, even ostracized life style he had chosen, he felt the need to justify his words and actions before mankind and--for his own peace of mind--before himself. Sure that his philosophy, his mode of life were the only right ones and, in order to convince his fellow man of it, he had to attempt the im-possible, the unimaginable feat of retrieving from the remotest regions of his existence every hidden emotion, every past action, from the most trivial to the most consequential. He had to bare his soul, turn it, so-to-speak, inside out, until there was not the smallest nook left in darkness. He had to expose its deepest secrets, its faint-est tremors, before he himself could believe and say to his fellow men with heartfelt conviction: I am innocent because I am virtuous. Rousseau, contrary to most previous autobiographers, did not write his *Confessions* for the sake of recording his life. He wrote them as a means to an end. And the end was self-justification.

The *Confessions* present the reader with a totally new concept of man, modern man, conscious of his uniqueness and therefore, of this alienation from society. And this man is not afraid to show his shortcomings as well as his virtues "in all sincerity." This in fact is, according to Rousseau, the singly most important aspect of his undertaking, to show *everything*, without dissimulation, without falsification, and above all, without omissions.

Since it is the purpose of this study to isolate and trace those elements in the various works which influenced the evolution of the autobiographical genre, Rousseau's insistence on absolute sincerity seems of special significance, because its reverberations (i.e., the trend for "sincere" disclosure of the most intimate detail) can be felt not only in future autobiographies, but throughout the Western literary tradition up to our present time. As we have seen in Chapter I, sincerity is one of the most essential aspects in our definition of the conventional autobiographer. Yet, none of Rousseau's prede-cessors had claimed to "tell all." They had judiciously exercised their right to omit those details and incidents which they felt were inconsequential in relation to their life or contrary to *bienséance*. That a man would, indeed, tell all and be completely sincere about it, is such an unprecedented occurrence that it deserves our attention. If Rousseau did adhere to this maxim throughout his work, then his autobiography is, in effect, the epitome of all autobiographies ever written. If, however, he reveals his life in all its glory and all its misery and *adapts* the presentation of the facts according to his objective--to write his apologia--then his work lays the groundwork for the identity crises of the genre. A close examination of several narrated experiences will put his sincerity to the test in order to see, whether he followed the conventions of the traditional autobiographer or whether his work is one of the first branchings off the established path.

Jean-Jacques Rousseau evoked probably more controversy and caused more polemics in the short span of ten years (1750-1760) than any other prominent writer did during an entire lifetime. The fear that his many powerful and outspoken "enemies"--real or imagined--would leave a distorted and unfavorable account of his life and actions to posterity prompted him to write his *Confessions*. He wanted to leave a portrait of the "real Jean-Jacques." Unlike Montaigne[3] he was not interested in describing the condition of his intellect or in pursuing the story of its development. His professed concern was the condition of his soul which, when everything had been told, would--at least so he hoped--testify to the natural goodness and innocence of Jean-Jacques Rousseau. The fact that he devoted his remaining years almost exclusively to the composition of additional autobiographical works[4] seems to point to an initial dissatis-

---

3 Montaigne, *Essais* in *Oeuvres Complètes*, Paris, Editions Gallimard, 1962.
4 Jean-Jacques Rousseau, *Les Confessions* (1766-1770), *Rousseau juge de Jean-Jacques* (1772-1776), and *Reveries du Promeneur solitaire* (1776-1778); Although Rousseau had collected autobiographical data and had written a number of drafts and sketches as many as seven years prior to 1766, the actual composition of the work as we have it today was started in 1766 during his sojourn at Wootton, England. For preliminary sketches and variants see Rousseau, *Les Confessions--Autres textes autobiographiques*, Paris, Editions Gallimard, 1959. All references--unless otherwise indicated--

faction with the *Confessions*.[5] Each of these works reflects his all en-compassing desire to justify himself, to convince the world and himself of his virtue and his innate goodness. To my knowledge no one before him had dared to bare his soul so completely, to drag to the fore the most sordid as well as the most sublime secrets and emotions hidden in the dark recesses of his existence. If Saint Augustine, his famous predecessor, had discretely admitted to fornication and his inability to resist the temptations of the flesh,[6] Jean-Jacques candidly claims to have fathered five children with his "servant," "governess," and later "hostess," children who were immediately after birth deposited at the steps of the public foundlings' home. "Everything considered I chose the best, or what I considered the best for my children," he tells his reader unabashedly some twenty years later, "I still wish I would have been raised and nourished as they were" (Rousseau, *Conf.* Bk. 8, p. 357). Minutely, almost graphically, Rousseau describes a variety of sexual experiences from the time he found intense gratification as a precocious youngster from a spanking administered by a not-so-young lady. He freely discusses his addiction to masturbation, his exhibitionism (Bk. 1-4), and his in-

are to this edition and will be given as follows: Rousseau, Bk. 3, p. 3. All translations are my own.

5   There are, of course, other speculations why Rousseau continued to write autobiographical works. Lester Crocker, who maintains that Rousseau wrote his *Confessions* in search of his identity, says: "Obviously, Rousseau never achieved a normal stage of identity. . . . He invented an imaginary role for himself as a prophetic voice, superior, but spurned and persecuted. For some years [presumably those surrounding the composition of the *Confessions*], he was able to maintain that fiction," cf. Lester G. Crocker, *Jean-Jacques Rousseau*, 2 vol., New York, The Macmillan Company, 1973, p. 193, vol. 2 –brackets are mine.

6   "And what was it," asks Saint Augustine, "that I delighted in, but love, and be loved? But I kept not the measure of love, of mind to mind, friendship's bright boundary: but out of the muddy concupiscence of the flesh, and the bubblings of youth, mists fumed up which beclouded and overcast my heart, that I could not discern the clear brightness of love from the fog of lustfulness. Both did confusedly boil in me, and hurried my unstayed youth over the precipice of unholy desires, and sunk me in the gulf of flagitiousnesses." *The Confessions of Saint Augustine*, tr. E.B. Pusey, New York, Random House, Inc., 1949, Bk 2, p. 24

volvement in a *ménage-à-trois* (Bk. 5). Saint Augustine confesses to the wanton ravaging of the neighbor's fruit trees and considers this act a sign of his unworthiness.[7] Jean-Jacques not only stole, but he accused another of this theft, knowing full well that this action, far from ameliorating his own position, jeopardized the very future of the young servant he had accused (Bk. 2, pp. 86-87). Unlike Saint Augustine, Jean-Jacques does not view this action as a sign a depravity, but rather the logical consequence of his lowly and degrading condition as an apprentice and servant, i.e., the inevitable result of social injustice.

In 1750, Rousseau—convinced of the veracity of his pronouncements made in his *Discours sur les sciences et les arts,* or inebriated by his own rhetoric—adopted the pose of the "naturally good and innocent" man. By the time he started to write his confessions, he had been acting this role for a decade and a half. He had convinced himself of his virtues.[8] "I envy the glory of the martyrs," he wrote in a letter to Saint Germain on February 26, 1770. "If I don't have quite the same belief as they do, I have the same innocence and the same zeal, and my heart feels worthy of the same prize."[9] And like the martyrs, he felt persecuted by real and imagined enemies who misinterpreted his actions because they were ignorant of the purity of his soul. In order to rectify this misunderstanding, to remove the tarnish from his name, Rousseau had to write his confessions, for which "absolute sincerity" was to be his only guideline.

---

7 "For I stole that, of which I had enough, and much better. Not cared I to enjoy what I stole, but joyed in the theft and sin itself. A pear tree there was near our vineyard, laden with fruit, tempting neither for colour nor taste. To shake this and rob this, some lewd young fellows of us went, late one night . . . and took huge loads, not for our eating, but to fling to the very hogs, having only tasted them." Saint Augustine, *op. cit.,* Bk. 2, p. 29.

8 A strong case could be made that Rousseau underwent a drastic and genuine moral reform and attempted henceforth to live a life commensurate with his newly found principles. A very thorough study of his writings, however, has convinced me that it was, indeed, a pose which allowed him to parade and peddle his "virtue and innocence."

9 L. Crocker, *op. cit.,* p. 324 ff., vol. 2.

An early draft of the opening paragraphs of the *Confessions* shows that Rousseau was fully conscious of the many pitfalls awaiting the prospective autobiographer:

> No man can write the story of a man's life except he himself. The workings of his mind, his real life, is known only to him, but in setting it down on paper, he disguises it. Under the pretext of telling his story, he embarks upon an apologia. He exhibits himself as he would wish other men to see him, and not at all as he is. At best, the most sincere are truthful more or less in what they are saying, but they lie in their reticences, and what they do not confess changes so much what they make a pretense of avowing that, by reason of recounting only one part of the truth, they tell us nothing.[10]

Rousseau ranks Montaigne as the "chief of these falsely sincere" because he "reveals his blemishes, but only such as are agreeable . . . . There is no man, " he assures us, "who does not have odious shortcomings." He, Rousseau, was going to show all of his. And yet, the very motive for his autobiography, his burning desire for justification, lured him ever deeper into a maze of deceptive passages, till he lost in the end all sense of the positive direction he so ardently desired to pursue.

Sometime around 1759 or 1760, before starting his autobiography, Rousseau had adopted the motto VITEM IMPENDERE VERO for his life.[11] It was to be the guiding light for his autobiography, when he set out to make his confession not before God, but before men, in order to be judged by them. For, contrary to Saint Augustine, it was the judgment of men that he feared. Thoroughly convinced of this innate goodness, he had no need to fear that of God.

> May the trumpet of the last judgment sound whenever it may; I shall present myself with this book in my hand before the sovereign judge. Loudly I shall proclaim: here is what I have done, what I have thought, and what I was. I have related the good and the bad with the same candor, and if it happened that I used some inconsequential ornament, it was

10 J.-J. Rousseau, *op. cit.*, p. 1149.
11 cf. Jean Guehénno, *Jean-Jacques Rousseau*, trans. J. and D. Weightman, London, Routledge & Kegan Paul, 1966, pp. 32-35.

only to fill a void caused by my faulty memory. . . . I have shown myself as I was, despicable and vile when I acted it, good, generous, and sublime, when I was that: I unveiled my soul just as You have seen it. Eternal Being assemble around me the innumerable crowd of my fellow beings: let them hear my confessions, let them sob over my indignities, let them blush over my miseries. May each one at his turn discover with the same sincerity his heart at the bottom of Your throne: and then, let a single one say if he dare: I was better than this man. (Rousseau, *Conf.* Bk. 1, p. 5.)

In this opening paragraph Rousseau speaks with the eloquence and the conviction of the righteously indignant, with the haughtiness and arrogance of the misunderstood, misjudged, and unappreciated prophet of a new man. The unique Jean-Jacques is about to make his unique confession, and the opening statement proclaims his defiant threat: beware of judging me lest you may be judged yourself! An aura of exhibitionism pervades the entire autobiography and threatens to involve the reader--who has become witness to this exhibitionism--in an act of complicity. Again and again the echoes of the opening statement resound throughout the work: I may be vile and blemished but I dare you to proclaim your innocence and purity!

Rousseau professes to be absolutely sincere (and what reader could question his visibly agonizing attempt at sincerity?) and he demands that the reader acknowledge his uniqueness in regard to his "unquestionable sincerity and utmost honesty" and grant him understanding, compassion, and finally absolution. Should he refuse to do so, should he retain the smallest trace of reservation in regard to Rousseau's innate virtue and goodness after having read this work, then indeed the reader himself is a scoundrel who "deserves to be done away with" (Rousseau, *Conf.*, Bk. 12, p. 656). Admittedly, this is a *tour-de-force* Rousseau is attempting, but he attempts it with all the determination he can muster. And he uses all the registers of human expression to succeed with it. Passages of biting or eloquent rhetoric are followed by quietly serene descriptions of places and events; the boisterous youth and the babbling dotard are there. The blurting out of embarrassing secrets is followed by vain attempts at justification.[12] Lester Crocker points out that Rousseau had to write

12 Montaigne claimed to be no less sincere when he said in 1580: "This here is

his *Confessions* as an intuitive act of self preservation, to justify himself to himself and against a hostile, impenetrable world. Having no other way to save himself, he had to find himself. He sought, according to Crocker, what he needed--not objective certainty, but subjective certainty.[13] His past life and actions had to substantiate the self he had been busy creating and cultivating ever since his "Illumination" in 1750. And though he may have found self-justification to a certain degree, his advancing paranoia--which bordered in its later stages on absolute madness--compelled the poor, haunted man to justify himself to himself forever anew for the rest of his remaining life.[14]

a book of good faith, reader . . . I want to be seen in my simple way, natural, and ordinary, without contention or artifice: for it is I whom I am painting". Montaigne, *op. cit.*, p. 9.

13 Lester G. Crocker, *op. cit.*, p. IX, vol. 1.

14 Started as a collection of twenty-four pages entitled "my portrait" (frequently referred to as "My Memoirs"), *The Confessions,* after an incubation period of almost ten years, started to take its final shape after repeated prodding and urging by his friends and publishers Rey, Moulton, and Duclos in 1764. The work was eagerly awaited by Rousseau's admirers, but his discarded friends and outspoken critics felt considerable apprehension and uneasiness when they heard about the planned work. Rousseau started actual composition in 1766 and put the finishing touches on it in Paris in 1770. While he had actually spent roughly ten years contemplating the project and collecting the necessary materials for Books one through six, he completed Books seven through twelve in a record time of roughly four months. The Geneva manuscript is preceded by a note to the reader in which Rousseau evaluates and criticizes part II of his work. "These books," he tells us, "are full of mistakes of all sorts . . . inferior in everything to the first part." He proceeds to explain that if the latter books are so much different in tone, color, poetic quality, and finally by their style, it is not only because of the contrast of his obscure youth and his present position as a well-known writer, but also because he is incapable of achieving the necessary distance between the very recent past which is tearing him apart and the uncertainty of a perilous future (Rousseau, *op. cit.*, p. XXXIX).

In his subsequent autobiographical writings Jean-Jacques' tone is considerably meeker. "If I would dare ask a favor of those who will hold these writings in their hands it would be that they would kindly read them in their entirety before putting them away or even before talking to someone about them. Anticipating that this wish will not be granted to me, I'll be

The *Confessions* terminate in the same tone of admonishment and threat as they begin:

> I have spoken the truth. If anyone knows the facts I have shown differently, had they been proven a thousand times, he knows lies and deceptions. And if he refuses to go to the bottom of these, trying to clear them up with me while I am still alive, then he loves neither justice nor truth. As for myself, I declare loudly and without fear: whoever, even without having read my works, shall examine with his proper eyes my nature, my character, my customs, my inclinations, my joys, my habits and could believe me to be a dishonest man, is a man who deserves to be strangled. (Rousseau, p. 56).

To hear such words, one cannot doubt the depth of Rousseau's attempt at absolute sincerity. But such a sincere attempt to find the truth, does not necessarily equal truth. The problem is that this man was too thoroughly convinced of his innate virtues and his goodness, and he felt that his heart, his innermost being, was utterly incapable of any felonious or malicious thought or action. Consequently he relived his entire life as we see it in the *Confessions* on this premise. This idea had become an obsession with him, obscuring any rational thought that might have kept him closer to the path of objective truth. His friends tolerated it benignly, his enemies made it the starting point of their often ferocious and malicious attacks. As it turned out, he became, despite his agonizing efforts, one of the "falsely sincere," showing us not what he was, but what he would have liked to be.[15] Every link in this enormous chain of life must support and

silent and leave everything up to Providence" (Preface to the Dialogues *Rousseau juge de Jean-Jacques, op. cit.*, p. 659). In the Dialogues between Rousseau and a fictive Frenchman, the author is looking for his "subjective certainty." Here he is trying to prove himself and–"Providence willing"--to the world that he was and had been the innocent victim of social injustice and a malicious cabal. In the *Reveries*, on the contrary, he finds moments of voluptuous bliss and serene tranquility turning inward and reliving his childhood and early youth which the passing of time had shrouded in an aura of perfect happiness, a condition which reality had never held for him.

15 Bernardin once asked Rousseau whether the *Nouvelle Heloïse* was not his own story. "It is not exactly what I have been," answered Rousseau, "but what I would have liked to be." cf. J.L. Lecercle, *Rousseau et l'art du roman*, Paris, Armand Colin, 1969, p. 119.

underline his basic statement: I am initially good, honest and sincere. I cannot be anything but good, and if I have ever done anything evil, it was not I, but some evil influence, some temporary madness or passion, fate, or my enemies which forced me to act contrary to my nature, and therefore I cannot be held responsible.[16]

When writing his *Confessions*, Rousseau wrote a book *à thèse*, a most fascinating picaresque novel whose hero developed and acted according to the philosophical pronouncements the writer had made after his legendary "illumination" under the oak tree on his way to Vincennes (Rousseau, *Conf.* p. 351), at age thirty-seven. Many events and actions of his previous life and of his succeeding years could not and cannot be reconciled with his so-called "reform-principles" (i.e. his return to a "natural" way of life) without a considerable stretching of the imagination or without the author appearing the hypocrite he so ardently fought not to be.[17]

It is not the purpose of this study to examine the twelve books of Rousseau's *Confessions*. Innumerable studies have been made to examine and illuminate the work from every conceivable angle of human endeavour (literary, political, social, pedagogical, even medical), from the most important and most decisive to the most insignificant incident and detail.[18] Case histories have been compiled on the

16 Blanchard in his analysis of the writer's paranoia tells us: "Rousseau's delusional system became a guarantee of his own innocence, of his right to Paradise." W.H. Blanchard, *Rousseau and the Spirit of Revolt*, Ann Arbor, Michigan Press, 1967, p. 184.

17 Let us not forget for one moment that the poet's moral reform was not effected until after he had received the Prize of the Academy of Dijon in 1750 for his *Discours sur les arts et les sciences*, which, because of its anti-progress and anti-civilization tenets, caused considerable polemics in and outside of France. It brought Rousseau almost over night the publicity and fame he had so doggedly striven for, ever since he first set foot into Paris in 1742. Also, his collaboration with the Encyclopedists, who epitomized knowledge, science, and progress, seems hard to reconcile with Rousseau's newly adopted anti-progress stance. By the same token, the success of his opera *Le devin du village* (1752), until then his crowning literary achievement, caused subsequently considerable embarrassment, for it was ill suited to complement the newly adopted image of a man who declared all theater performances frivolous and downright immoral.

18 The editors of the Pléiade Edition, Bernard Gagnebin and Marcel Raymond,

50

writer's genius, his literary innovations, his sicknesses, his sexual potence or impotence, his masochism and perversions.[19] Unwilling to believe that a man would and could tell all, scholars searched public and private archives to prove the *Confessions* fictional, or worse, the fantasies of a sick mind. They found to their surprise (or satisfaction) countless documents supporting almost every single factual statement mentioned in the work. The few chronological errors seem at first glance insignificant and pardonable, especially in view of the author's stated intention of recording the state of his soul and not any specific events. Making use of this vast compilation, I shall isolate and examine a few links in the long chain of events recorded by Rousseau in order to put his much publicized sincerity to the test. The chosen examples will show how easily objective truth can be subjectified merely by the slant of presentation or by an "insignificant" chronological "error," and how easily the autobiographer himself, despite all precautions and apprehensions, can be misled if he starts his autobiography with an additional, specific objective in

included in their notes most of the factual data available on Rousseau, no matter whether it was in agreement or disagreement with the recorded events in the *Confessions.* Other recent works of particular interest are those of Jean Guehénno, *op. cit.,* J. Starobinski (*J.-J. Rousseau: La transparence et l'obstacle,* Paris, Colin, 1958), J.L. Lecercle (*Rousseau et l'art du roman,* Paris, Colin, 1969) and L.G. Crocker, *op. cit.,* who summarizes a considerable amount of previous studies in his excellent two volume work on Rousseau.

19 cf. L. J. Courtois, *Enfance faubourienne ou Jean-Jacques à Coutance,* Geneva, 1933. Robert Dottrens, "Jean-Jacques Rousseau educateur," in *Jean-Jacques Rousseau,* Neuchatel, Université ouvriers et Faculté des Lettres de l'Université de Génève, 1962. Louis Dufour-Vernes, *Recherches sur J.-J. Rousseau et sa parenté,* Génève, 1878. Charles Eisenmann "La Cité de Jean-Jacques Rousseau," in *Etudes sur le Contrat Social de J.-J. Rousseau,* Paris, Societé les Belles Lettres, 1964. René LaForgue, *Psycho-pathologie de l'échec,* Paris, 1944 (Chap. IX "Jean-Jacques Rousseau"). Ronald Grimsley, *Rousseau and the Religious Quest,* Oxford, 1968. Th. Heyer, "Une inscription relative à J.-J. Rousseau," in *Memoirs et Documents publiés par la Société d'Histoire et d'Archéologie de Génève,* Vol. IX, 1855, pp. 409-420. Eugene Ritter, *La Famille et la jeunesse de J.-J. Rousseau,* Paris, 1896. Jean Starobinski, "The Illness of Rousseau," *Yale French Studies, No.* XXVIII, pp. 64-74.

mind, besides that of recording the story of his life. Such a subjectified version certainly cannot disprove Rousseau's attempted sincerity, it merely adds another dimension, one that the writer attempted so desperately to conceal, to the character and the all-too-human weaknesses of the protagonist.

Rousseau's *à-thèse* development becomes apparent from the very first pages of the *Confessions* where he describes the very touching love story of the childhood sweethearts destined to become his parents. The rich, beautiful girl meets a poor, virtuous boy. Tender love, mutual esteem, virtue and perseverance help them overcome such obstacles as parental objection and forced separation. When the girl's brother discovers his love for the boy's sister and the foursome receives its nuptial blessings on the very same day, the picture of familial harmony and bliss seems perfect. These very same people as well as his "mie Jacqueline," the family's gentle, friendly maid, surround and caress little Jean-Jacques after his mother's untimely death. (She died from childbed fever after Jean-Jacques' birth, but her memory was lovingly kept alive by those who cared for the infant.) The author seems perfectly justified in asking himself (and at the same time the reader): "How could I have become wicked, when I never saw anything but models of virtue and gentleness around me?"

The historical facts, however, differ slightly: Jean-Jacques' uncle and aunt had been married in 1699, his parents in 1704. In 1695 (i.e. nine years prior to her marriage) his beautiful mother was in love, not with Isaac, her future husband, but with a well-known and well-respected gentleman in Geneva, a M. Sarasin, who was already married and a father. Jean-Jacques mentions that duty called his father to Constantinople as watchmaker to the serail, but that his mother's entreaties brought back her loving husband, "abandoning everything" (Rousseau, *Conf.* Bk. 1, p. 7). The fact is that after one year of married bliss and the birth of his oldest son, Isaac "the honest watchmaker" became restless. He left his wife and son to seek his fortune elsewhere. He did not return until six years later. In the *Confessions* we hear nothing about the violent temper which often made life difficult and miserable for the children and the servant.[20]

20 cf. Eugene Ritter, *La Famille et la Jeunesse de J.-J. Rousseau*, Paris, 1896,

Jean-Jacques prefers to overlook the complete neglect of the children's early education (which seemed to consist primarily of reading the seventeenth century novels and romances left by his mother) and the lack of paternal guidance and supervision which turned his brother François into a "scamp and good-for-nothing," whom he, Jean-Jacques "nevertheless always loved most tenderly."[21] Fortunately the brother-in-law, to whom Isaac seemed to have relegated his paternal duties, attempted at least to provide a semblance of education for Jean-Jacques—with the money left by his mother.

Psychologists, for whom Rousseau's life has provided a very fertile field of study, have seen the root of most of Jean-Jacques' emotional as well as physical problems in the extraordinary circumstances of his early childhood.[22] But for Jean-Jacques, writing his *Confessions* in exile in England, these were the happy, the good years of his life, full of love, mutual care and tenderness, freedom from cares and worries. This had been his Eden from whence he was driven, through no fault of his own.

In all fairness, we may assume that Rousseau knew nothing of these facts, since brought to light through the painstaking research of persistent scholars. He may have simply related the story the way he remembered it from a reminiscing father, aunt, or Nanny. Early childhood events are usually buried in the far recesses of our memories and they become too easily distorted over the years. Why should Rousseau have been an exception? And hadn't he told the reader of "insignificant ornaments" he would provide whenever memory failed him? Obviously this isolated incident is not sufficient proof that Jean-Jacques, pursuing his apologetic objective, consciously and deli-

also Louis Defour-Vernes, *Recherches sur J.-J. Rousseau et sa Parenté*, Geneva, 1878.

21 François, seven years older than Jean-Jacques, placed in a correctional institution at thirteen, ran away from his apprenticeship and was never heard of again. cf. also Rousseau, *op. cit.* notes by the editors p. 1238.

22 "It is impossible not to see that from his youth he showed the symptoms of neuroses." Gagnebin and Raymond, editors, Rousseau, *op. cit.* p. 1250. Of particular interest are also J. Starobinski's studies: *Rousseau: La transparence et l'obstacle*, Paris, Armand Colin, 1958.

berately altered the facts to coincide with his view of himself and the world and to arouse the reader's sympathy and compassion.[23] Yet, this is exactly what he did. One sole example would not prove that Rousseau, who prided himself on his remarkable memory, suffered deliberate memory lapses whenever it suited his intentions, that he used wiles and literary conventions alike in order to place Jean-Jacques in a position most advantageous, most suited to evoke compassion or pity from the reader. In order to support my contention and to put the author's sincerity further to the test, we shall examine three more similar incidents from the multitude in the *Confessions*.

After Jean-Jacques had received a very minimal amount of schooling with the Pastor and Mlle. Lambercier at Bossey, Rousseau's uncle, who had taken in hand the boy's education, decided that Jean-Jacques should learn a trade. An apprenticeship agreement was signed in 1725 with the very young master engraver, Abel Ducommun. Jean-Jacques at the time was barely thirteen years old. Inexperienced, gruff, and violent, the master demanded from his apprentices discipline, obedience, and submission, aspects of life completely alien to Jean-Jacques' upbringing. Step by step, Rousseau describes in the *Confessions* the "inevitable" and gradual deterioration of his moral character during the three years of his apprenticeship. Growing envy, indolence, theft, and lies are becoming his daily companions. But the naturally good Jean-Jacques is not responsible for these adverse developments. Rather, it is his treatment at the hands of his master, the companionship of his coarse fellow-apprentices, that are changing him. "Envy and helplessness," he tells us, "always lead to this. That is why all servants are scoundrels." The basic inequality and, in this case, tyranny of the master justify his vices, as far as he is concerned. And when he runs away from the town, it was only the master's and not the unruly apprentice's fault. Had the master been waiting for him, anxious that no harm had come to his

---

23 Since Rousseau frequently refers to Montaigne's *Essais*, he surely must have been familiar with the latter's statement that the easiest way to soften the hearts of those one has offended (especially when vengeance is in their hands and one finds oneself at their mercy) is to move them by submission to commiseration and pity. cf. Montaigne, *op. cit.*, p. 11.

young protegé during his nightly absence, Jean-Jacques surely would have returned to the shop, as soon as the town gates were opened in the morning. Endless and pathetic are his subjunctive incantations:

> I would have spent a peaceful and agreeable life in the midst of my religion, of my country, of my family, and of my friends, such as conformed to my personality, in the uniformity of a job according to my taste, and friends according to my heart. I would have been a good citizen, good father of a family, good friend, good worker, a good man in all things. I would have liked my condition, maybe honored it. And, after having passed an obscure and simple life, smooth and agreeable, I would have died peacefully at the bosom of my family. Soon forgotten, without a doubt, they would at least have missed me as long as they remembered me.

But fate had other plans for him. "The tyranny" of his master finally made work, which he "would have loved" intolerable for him. It gave him vices which he otherwise would have hated (Rousseau, *Conf.*, Bk. 1, p. 44).

The description of this particular episode in his life is another typical example of Rousseau's dominating theme, which already constituted the basic premise of his *Discours sur les sciences et les arts* in 1750: it is society and its institutions that make man evil. By 1766 he had become obsessed with it and it served as the justifying factor for all his vices and personal depravity. But in his obsession, Rousseau overlooks the fact that such an excuse cannot apply to his raiding of Monsieur Malby's wine cellar, for M. Malby had always treated him with due respect and even entrusted him with the keys to the cellar. It is also a rather poor excuse for the ribbon story, this inconsequential theft, explained with so much pomp and circumstance, so much *mea culpa*. Did he steal it, because he was a servant? because Mme. de Versellis had not taken the trouble to discover his "true value"? as an act of retribution, because M. Sagran had stolen his ribbon? or maybe because the dying lady had omitted him after barely three months of service from her testament? All of these reasons seem implied, but more cogently the reader gets the impression that once the evil seed had been implanted in a "naturally good human being" it could never be eradicated.

When Rousseau wrote his *Confessions*, he was a mature man, able to judge, to evaluate persons and situations. One wonders whether the thought ever crossed his mind that his master's age--he was just twenty years old--and the young man's preoccupations, cares, and worries with his business and a young family (facts significantly omitted from the *Confessions*) offered any extenuating circumstances. Probably not. If it did, Rousseau was most careful to omit any such indication from his autobiography. Instead, he assures his readers that his violent master "succeeded in a short time to tarnish all the brightness of his youth, to brutalize his loving and lively personality, and to reduce him in mind and fortune to the true state of an apprentice" (Rousseau, *Conf.*, p. 30). Yes, Jean-Jacques tells us, I did lie, and steal, and loaf, I did all these things, but they did not come naturally to me. They were forced upon me. All his perversions, or almost all of them, his various idiosyncrasies and peculiarities, he traces back to these years. His love of day-dreaming is one of them. This love for "imaginary objects and the facility to occupy myself with them led me," so he tells us, "to despise everything around me and awakened my taste for solitude." Another example is his misanthropic disposition which is nothing but "the effect of too affectionate, too loving, too tender a heart, which through lack of a corresponding counterpart is forced to nourish itself upon fiction" (Rousseau, *Conf.*, Bk. 1, p. 41). Jean-Jacques is plainly the victim of this terrible and undeserved situation, and who dare condemn him for fending for himself the best he could!

Jean-Jacques has vowed to tell the reader the whole truth about himself. And he tried to abide by his promise. Yet, where others sinned by omission, Jean-Jacques sins by his overriding desire to justify every one of his vices, every little transgression against a basically bourgeois code of morality. His I'll-show-you-that-I-am-innocent-attitude must be at the basis of occasional memory lapses and confusion, otherwise we'd have to accuse the man, who--just like Wordsworth--prided himself on an infallible memory, of deliberate dishonesty and fraud. The following episode is another such case in question.

After Rousseau had run away from his place of apprenticeship in Geneva, well-meaning strangers directed the errant young man to the safe haven of Madame de Warens at Annecy. Almost instantly forgotten were the trials and tribulations endured at the hands of Monsieur Ducommun. Here, indeed was the lovely, benevolent lady of his dreams welcoming the handsome young man with open arms into her home and her heart, introducing him step by step to the way of life and social conventions of the upper middle class and lesser nobility. Lovingly he draws her resplendent portrait, untarnished by later disappointments and deceptions. It was a sunny Palm Sunday when he met Madame, a young and radiantly beautiful divorcee, his savior, his angel, his "maman", for the first time. When he first saw her, she was about to enter the house of worship. What a promising sign for a new beginning! Palm Sunday, smiling skies, and a beautiful young woman. Their first encounter must have left an indelible impression. His devotion, nay, veneration for her never waned during the entire thirteen year period during which she intermittently kept him. He always speaks of Mme. de Warens with love and respect. Despite the innumerable hurts and humiliations he must have endured not only during their *ménage-à-trois* with Claude Anet, her valet and handyman, but especially when it became apparent that the good lady tried desperately to rid herself of the no longer welcome but, nevertheless, permanent guest, he never ceased to show his gratitude. It is possible that Jean-Jacques realized that Mme de Warens' already meager resources were unduly strained by his continued presence. But again and again, after every unsuccessful venture out into the world, he made his way back to her. She provided the necessary calm and gentleness, the necessary time to heal the latest wounds that society never ceased to inflict upon his pride and self-esteem. Initially sent to her for religious conversion (a convert herself, she maintained her home and supported herself with a royal pension accorded to her for just this purpose), he "became hers instantly, convinced that a religion preached by such missionaries could only lead to paradise" (Rousseau, *Conf.* Bk. 2, p. 49).

Writing this *apologia*, Rousseau undertook to write that of Mme. de Warens at the same time. From the very first moment of their encounter he venerated her as his benefactress, his maman. Their short amorous and, for the young man blissful, interlude at Les Charmettes provided the writer throughout his life with a source of endlessly pleasurable, serene, and nostalgic memories. His often unbelievably naive explanations and justifications for her weaknesses and shortcomings are indeed touching and testify to his unabating loyalty and devotion.[24] After having achieved fame and renown, after having found access to the most fashionable circles in Paris, he undoubtedly realized how much he owed to her influence, her generosity, and kindness. "I meet Mme. de Warens. This period of my life determined my character."[25] Well built, "timid, lovable, always afraid to displease," with no sense whatsoever for social conventions, and a knowledge which, far from being helpful, intimidated him only more and made him "feel more acutely, how much he lacked" (Rousseau, *Conf.*, Bk. 2, p. 48). Such is the picture of the errant teenager as he presented himself to Madame de Warens on this memorable Palm Sunday. It was maman's patient and thorough apprenticeship which gave him the basic rudiments for almost any social situation. From all indications it seems that the awareness of his uniqueness, his ever-increasing insistence on this uniqueness, his "special" station in life, as well as his contempt for the "*canaille*" are accompanying aspects of the education he received at Annecy. For no matter how widely acclaimed Rousseau, the writer and philosopher, is for his compassionate pleas for the suppressed, Rousseau, the individual, reserved his friendship and esteem exclusively for the nobility and a select group of famous people. His endless tirades for justice, his

24 "She was for me more than a sister, more than a mother, more than a friend, even more than a mistress . . . I loved her too much to desire her." All her faults, according to Rousseau, resulted from errors, never from passion or baseness. "When she made a choice [of lover] which did not do her much credit, it was not from base penchants which never came close to her noble heart, it was only from her too generous heart, too humane, too compassionate, too sensitive, that she did not always use enough discernment" (Rousseau, *Conf.*, Bk. 5, pp. 196-198).

25 There is an obvious discrepancy in this statement, when we consider how determining M. Ducommun's influence supposedly was upon his life. But then the *Confessions* abound in contradictions. In his third letter to Malesherbes Rousseau writes: "I did not start living until April 9, 1756" [the time he installed himself at the Hermitage]. But writing about this same time in the *Confessions* he says: "sighing, I cried out at times: Ah, this here [the Hermitage] is not Les Charmettes!" Yet when Mme. de Warens had "exiled" him to Les Charmettes when she had found herself a new lover, Rousseau became "mortally ill." When he left Chambery and Les Charmettes, he was cured as if by magic. cf. also Lecercle, *op. cit.*, p. 15.

clamoring for equality were prompted by the personal indignities he endured, the miseries he, the free citizen of Geneva, suffered at the hands of an assorted number of "*sots*," scoundrels, and hypocrites, who happened to be his superiors, not by a compassionate concern for the suppressed multitudes. It was his injured pride which led him to rant against the rich who, fascinated by his rebellious rantings, put up with his abuses and provided him and his *ménage* with all the necessities and a number of luxuries of life for many years.[26]

I have tried to show that Jean-Jacques owed Mme. de Warens considerable gratitude and, contrary to his attitude toward the greatest number of his benefactors (who sooner or later managed to arouse his wrath), he acknowledged it. In his most lyrical effusion he insists on his undying loyalty:

> That I could enshrine this happy place [where he first met her] with a golden gate! That I could arouse the veneration for it from the entire world! Whoever likes to honor the monuments of man's salvation should approach it only on his knees. (Rousseau, *Conf.*, p. 49, brackets are mine)

Mme. de Warens supplied him with all the financial, moral, and most importantly, the psychological support she could muster. And, unless she was indeed an angel in human form, one wonders where she found the patience and understanding to put up with Jean-Jacques' failures, his indolence, his sicknesses, his neuroses during thirteen long years.

From the multitude of events which left their marks upon Rousseau, some insignificant, some of apocalyptic nature, I shall concentrate on two--one at the beginning and one at the end of the Waren's period--to show how a "slight chronological error," the omission of a very trivial and "insignificant" fact served to project a so-much-more favorable personality trait of the author, bringing into focus

---

26 cf. for example what he had to say in regard to other unfortunates who came to seek Mme. des Warens' assistance: "she was forced by the priests to share her pension of 2,000 francs given to her by the king of Sardinia, with the rabble that came to sell its faith" (Rousseau, *Conf.*, p. 47). Could he have possibly overlooked the irony of such a statement, when a number of years earlier, he had gone through the same motions?

once more his acute sense of right and wrong, his "innate goodness."

After Rousseau had spent a few days in the tender, loving company of Mme. de Warens, the young heretic was sent to Turin for conversion. Maman, despite her reluctance to let him part, could not, in all propriety insist on retaining the youth. He was sent off, with the proper chaperons, on another one of his legendary pedestrian travels.

After having narrated his thoroughly enjoyable journey to Turin, the author pauses and asks the reader's indulgence for recording all these minor details, but, he says

> the endeavour I engaged in, to show myself completely to the public, demands that nothing about me must remain obscure or hidden; I must keep myself before my own eyes incessantly, advance in all the recesses of my heart, in all the nooks of my life, so that the reader may not lose me from sight for one instant, from fear of finding in my story the smallest break. He would then ask himself: what did he do during that time, and accuse me of not having told everything. (Rousseau, *Conf.*, p. 59).

The obvious reason for dwelling on his sincerity at that point is doubtless the fact that the story of his conversion had become for the proud citizen of Geneva a source of utter embarrassment.[27] In an effort of rehabilitation and revenge, everything and everyone connected with it--excepting, of course, Mme. de Warens--is described in the most sinister colors, under the most villainous aspects. His guides, pleasant enough during the journey, relieved him of every little bit of his meager possessions, his last penny, even a bit of "silver-encrusted ribbon," given to him by maman for his "little sword." Upon his arrival in Turin, he was instantly led to the hospice "in order to be taught the religion for which they sold me my sustenance" (*Conf.*, Bk. 2, p. 60). His account depicts the moral character of the inhabitants of the hospice, heretics and priests alike, and of the ominous procedures followed by the latter to convert the former.

Again the narrative is interrupted to emphasize the "intelligent and healthy education" he had received, the "lessons of wisdom and

---

27 "Jean-Jacques," says Crocker, "was deeply unbearably ashamed all his life of his double defection--from religion and country . . . he excuses it by assuring us that he had no intention to do either" (L. Crocker, *op. cit.*, p. 50).

examples of honor" he witnessed as a child within a family of utmost merit, instilling in the child by word and deed his "distinguishing principles of piety" (Rousseau, *Conf.*, p. 61), as well as his horror of "all things catholic." It is no surprise that, in order to ease his conscience, the now fifty-four year old Rousseau associated "papistry" in his *Confessions* strictly with amusement and "gourmandise" of a youth, acquiesing in order to eat.

Eight pages are devoted to his stay at the hospice. The most villainous, dishonest, and perverse, the very scum of humanity seems assembled in the halls of the hospice, and there is no reason to doubt the veracity of the diverse character portraits. The situation changes radically, however, when Rousseau paints the picture of his own valors and sagacity. Young as he was, he outwits the most adept of the converters in theological arguments. And as for the Fathers of the Church, he knows them at least as intimately as his opponents. He holds his grounds valiantly, but his adversaries, cunning and conniving, are at a definite advantage, having at their disposition all the resources of the entire Catholic Church, while he, the young, inexperienced lad, alone in an alien environment and country had nothing but his virtue and his unerring heart to fall back upon. One after the other of the other heretics was baptized. Only Jean-Jacques prevailed. It took the directors another month to complete this difficult conversion.

Again research has substantiated practically all of the facts as far as they could be verified, with one exception: the length of Jean-Jacques' stay at the hospice. The records of the Hospice du San Spirito at Turin show that Rousseau entered April 12, abjured April 21, and was baptized on April 23, when he presumably left the place in a hurry, for he was not signed out. This would, indeed, mean a record conversion, the average catucheme taking between three to six weeks before being baptized. Had he erred by a week or even two, the discrepancy would not be as startling. But Jean-Jacques makes it a point to tell us that it took the directors of the hospice three months to convert him. What other purpose could he have had in falsifying the time element involved, except to show that his conversion was not a light-hearted act of a carefree and unthinking youth, but his final capitulation in a valiant struggle where all the odds were against him.

The other incident underlining his innate goodness and virtue, and just as revealing as the preceding one, occurred during the final months of his stay with Mme. de Warens. It was all the more upsetting for Jean-Jacques (now twenty-five years old) since it followed only one year after his idyllic interlude with Maman at les Charmettes. Over the years Maman's financial situation had been getting progressively worse. She had been forced to move to more modest quarters in Chambery, where Jean-Jacques had joined her again in 1731. Engaged in a variety of unsuccessful business ventures, she employed Jean-Jacques for all sorts of errands, always on the lookout for a suitable position for her protegé. By then Jean-Jacques had definitely renounced learning a trade[28] and after Claude Anet's mysterious death (Claude had been his partner in their *ménage-à-trois*) his position near and with maman seemed permanently assured. Totally dependent on her, he made himself useful and agreeable in a thousand different ways. Apart from his increasingly frequent bouts with sickness he spent "the most serene and happy years of his life" traveling, studying, pursuing his music, and occasionally herbalizing. In 1735-36 maman had acquired a house in the country--Les Charmettes--and it was there that their life of serene tranquility reached its climax. As early as 1737, however, when Jean-Jacques was absent on a business trip, a robust young man, Winzenried-Courtilles, appeared on the scene. Rather than accepting another arrangement similar to the one with Claude, Rousseau preferred exile at Les Charmettes, the solitude of his studies to the company of the "wig-maker" at Chambery. Again he believed himself fatally ill, and the famous Dr. Fizes in Montpellier seemed to be the only hope for his recovery. In the *Confessions,* Rousseau speaks freely about his stay at Les Charmettes and his solitary pursuits. But significantly enough, he avoids to mention Winzenried's presence at Mme. de Waren's place prior to his de-

---

28 Guehénno maintains that Rousseau had taken such a decision at a much earlier date: "The truth is that from his thirteenth year onwards he inevitably resented the business of working for profit as a form of constraint. He was by nature one of those men for whom earning a living is not enough. Their real work is to be idle; to think thoughts and dream dreams, and they are impatient of anything which distracts their attention from it." Jean Guehénno, *op. cit.*, vol. 2, p. 15.

parture to Montpellier. Rather, the reader is given the impressions, that it was maman's concern and anguish that determined him to seek a cure from Dr. Fizes.

On his way to Montpellier Rousseau made the acquaintance of the vivacious widow, Mme. de Larnage. In the company of this temperamental lady, his illness disappeared miraculously and he enjoyed a passionate affair with her. When he arrived at Montpellier, the good doctor could find nothing wrong with the patient. In Rousseau's correspondence we find letter after letter written to maman imploring, begging asking for forgiveness, agreeing to any condition if she would just take him back. But maman was negligent in responding. And when he finally did receive a reply, it was most evasive. Of course, none of these letters, not even the incertitude which prompted him to cut short his intended stay are mentioned in the *Confessions*. But he does tell us how he avoided temptation (i.e. an invitation to spend more time with Mme. de Larnage), making instead a resolution to "expiate his trespasses, to arrange his behavior according to the laws of virtue, and to consecrate himself to the service of the best of all mothers, to bring to her the same amount of fidelity as he had shown devotion." What reader can remain indifferent to such a show of loyalty and devotion on the part of the young man? Who is not compelled to exclaim: Ah, here, indeed, is true virtue! But Rousseau's good intentions came all to naught. His return to Chambery was--especially in view of his good intentions–an absolute and irrevocable catastrophe. No one welcomed him home. Quite obviously, he was not expected to return to what he considered his "home." Maman advised him calmly that his place had been taken by Winzenried. Once again, his fate had been sealed. Again, he was exiled from paradise.

A very touching account, indeed, with very dramatic staging and effect. The fact that Rousseau did not mention Winzenried's presence before he left, nor the humiliating letters he wrote, makes the experience all the more dramatic. He did not hesitate to talk at length about his love affair with the passionate redhead–by his own admission the only one he ever enjoyed in his life–on the contrary, he emphasizes all its alluring aspects. How much clearer does this bring out his innate virtue, his basic decency, when in the face of temptation (to follow Mme. de Larange's invitation) he remembers where his loyalty ought to be; how much more ennobling the resolutions made on his return trip, and how much more ignoble the behavior of those who deceived him? The omission of this very insignificant detail (Winzenried's presence before his departure) serves again—just like his apprenticeship experience—to support Rousseau's initial premise, to present himself in a most favorable light in order to evoke the reader's compassion and forgiveness.

I have chosen four instances in order to demonstrate how skillfully Rousseau "in all sincerity" manipulated events in order to elicit maximum reader reaction. In a most subtle and inconspicuous way the circumstances are molded to conform to the *à-thèse* development of Jean-Jacques Rousseau. When the author assured us that he was going to write his confessions, not his justification (*Conf.*, Bk. 8, p. 359) he probably believed it in all sincerity. But he did end up writing his justification.

> I was sure that across my faults and weaknesses, despite my inability to carry any yoke, one would always find a just and good man, without spite, without hate, without jealousy, ready to recognize his wrongdoings, readier to forget those of others, seeking his sole happiness in the loving and gentle passions, bringing to all things a sincerity bordering on imprudence, to the point of the most incredible unselfishness. (*Conf.*, Bk. 12, p. 639)

This is, indeed, the man Rousseau intended to show in his *Confessions*. This is the man he, indeed, believed himself to be. But is this the real Jean-Jacques? Or was there another one full of haughtiness, intolerance, petty jealousy and spite, who forever quarrelled with friends and foes alike? And if there was another one, which one was the real Jean-Jacques? "He was not the martyr he believed himself to be," says Guehénno, "but he hankered after a martyr's halo." And Lecercle tells us: "Indeed he dreams his life and he dreams Jean-Jacques." But where else, if not in his autobiography, could we find the real Jean-Jacques? "I am writing less the history of events in themselves, as that of the conditions of my soul as they come about," tells us the autobiographer. And he would have succeeded in doing just that, had his ulterior motive not intervened. As it is, he gave the reader no chance to decide what he thought of Jean-

Jacques; instead he was told what he had better think. The author was so thoroughly convinced of his virtue and honesty, he refused to consider the possibility that anyone might not be impressed by it. To a very long-standing and faithful friend, Madame De La Tour-Franqueville—not even mentioned in his *Confessions*—he, the professed lover of mankind, once wrote: "Whoever is not passionately fond of me is unworthy of me," and he continued with equal haughtiness, "a person may not care for my books, I have no fault with that; but whoever does not love me because of my books is a knave."[29]

M. Beebe seems to have misunderstood Rousseau at least on one point when he wrote that the writer's motive of *The Confessions* was to attain peace and harmony through self-understanding and self-acceptance and to discover a means of escape from the conflict between his heart and his mind.[30] The fact is, there was no conflict. Rousseau's ratio merely provided the logical explanation and justification for any act that might have been prompted by his heart. A man who can matter-of-factly admit that he abandoned his five children at the foundling home (three of which were born when he lived in relative ease and comfort in a house in the country) and succeeds in convincing himself that it was the right and only thing to do, such a man must have a strangely distorted mind or a rather calloused heart. Jean-Jacques had no problem understanding himself, only in making himself understood. His conflict was not within himself, it was with the real world, with friends and foes. Rather, he was inebriated by his virtue, an egomaniac in love with himself, and it was during the moments of solitude when he submerged himself into his own soul, intoxicating himself with fond reveries, that he found the desired harmony and happiness he could not find in real life.

When Rousseau set out to write his autobiography, he pointed to the uniqueness of his endeavour. He did not exaggerate. He was the first writer to secularize the confession, to bare his soul in front of his fellow men to a point that would have horrified even Saint

29 Quoted by C.A. Sainte-Beuve, *Portraits of the Eighteenth Century*, tr. K. Wormerly, New York and London, G.P. Putnam's Sons, 1905, p. 140.
30 Maurice Beebe, *Ivory Towers and Sacred Founts*, New York, University Press, 1964, p. 43.

Augustine. He exposed aspects of human depravity, perversity, and squalor that never before had found a place in autobiography. He brought to the autobiographical genre the language bordering frequently on the sublime, a prose more lyrical than most exquisite poetry. And above all, he initiated *le culte du soi* which found numerous adherents not only among the Romanticists, but among writers well into the twentieth century.[31] With his extreme sensibility, the description and analysis of the faintest tremor of his soul, he gave us "the first fully developed self-portrait of the artist in modern literature."[32] But his sincerity, despite all his claims, was not always genuine or consistent. He manipulated it most ingeniously to make it coincide so perfectly with his *created* personality and character and, therefore, with his underlying objective, that he succeeds in convincing most readers both of his sincerity and of the uniqueness of his individuality.

I have pointed out before that Rousseau *almost* convinced himself that he was, indeed, the man he presented to his readers in the *Confessions*. But just almost. Had he found the self-justification he was seeking, had he been able to fully accept his new self as a logical outcome of his previous life and experiences, then he would not have felt any need for these subtle little distortions. Above all, he would have felt no further need for additional autobiographical writings. Rousseau had a vision of the perfect, the "natural man." It was his mania to think that he was that man. And he gave us his life distorted by his mania, as he liked to see it. He may repel his reader with his false humility, his masochistic tendencies, which he parades through his work with the same indecent exhibitionism he practiced in the streets of Paris. Yet, at the same time, he fascinates us. Maybe because, as François Maurois pointed out, "he is one of us. This master of deceit and pride finds among us his true faithfuls . . . We love him as we love ourselves, we hate him as we hate ourselves."

Jean-Jacques' undertaking was indeed as unique as he claimed it to be. No one had ever dared to throw off clothing and dressing alike so that we may stare–and maybe marvel––not only at the man's nakedness, but also at his innumerable bruises, cuts, and cancerous

31 cf. L. Crocker, J.L. Lecercle, J. Guehénno, *op. cit.*
32 M. Beebe, *op. cit.*, p. 39.

growths, his infirmities and his squalor. Ecce homo! His autobiography is in many respects the true portrait of the real Rousseau. We only have to compare it with some of his letters, where, as L. Crocker has pointed out, "we witness the same admixture of desperation and deceit, of the pleading and the admonitory, of degradation, and the parade of superior virtue."[33] These letters reflect the same underlying motive as the autobiography: self-justification, and their basic premise is: I am good.

In March 1770, after the completion of the *Confessions*, he wrote to Mme. de Berthier:

> You have esteemed me for my writing. You would esteem me even more for my life if it were known to you and even more for my heart, if it were open to your eyes. Never was there a heart more tender, better, or more just. Neither wickedness nor hatred has ever touched it. Certainly I have great vices, but they have never hurt anyone except me. . . . Remember three words with which I finish my adieux: I AM INNOCENT.[34]

From 1750 on, Rousseau had affected a pose. At age thirty-eight he decided that he was going to be the simple, virtuous, and natural (i.e. uncorrupted) man he had envisioned in his prize-winning *Discours*. By the time he started to write his *Confessions*, he was convinced that his present life-style and actions were sufficient proof that he was that man. Some past actions simply had to be modified slightly, in order to conform with his new image. There is no division between narrator and protagonist here, of the sort Professor Spengemann sees in Saint Augustine, the old Jean-Jacques and the regenerated one. There is only one narrator who relives and sees his life strictly in accordance with the premise that he is and was by nature innocent and good. Saint Augustine asks: "What man is he, who, weighing his own infirmity, dares to ascribe his purity and innocency to his own strength."[35] Jean-Jacques, preoccupied with himself to the point of excluding everything else, was that man. But the return upon himself did not only yield for Rousseau the certitude of his

---

33 L. Crocker, *op. cit.*, p. 321.
34 *Ibid.*, p. 321.
35 Saint Augustine, *op. cit.*, p. 32.

purity and innocence, it made him an extremely sensitive and more creative writer, for his art manifests itself most distinctly in his *Confessions* (Book 1-6) and his *Reveries du Promeneur solitaire.*

CHAPTER III

WILLIAM WORDSWORTH 1770-1850

Wordsworth's *Prelude* is, in its own way, every bit as unique as Rousseau's *Confessions*. Not only did Wordsworth introduce a totally novel objective to the writings of autobiography, but he contributed a host of new elements which determined the future scope (i.e. form and content) of similar works. It was the multiplicity and complexity of the poet's objective in *The Prelude* that was most instrumental to the evolution of the autobiography as well as to its inevitable division. We have seen the extent to which Rousseau's contribution to the genre had been determined by his objective. In order to justify himself, he had decided to show himself *à nu*, had dwelt on the condition of his soul and on his own particular individuality in its abjection and its glory. And because of his objective he had—despite his claim to the contrary—frequently violated the autobiographer's primary obligation to sincerity, changing historical reality to coincide with or to support his basic tenets. Wordsworth's main objectives were considerably more complex. The main thrust of his endeavor was no longer directed at the recording of his life. He was primarily interested in writing a literary masterpiece, and he accomplished his goal by tracing his own intellectual and spiritual growth, the development of a poet. Where Rousseau in his effort to justify himself had attempted to show society's adverse effects upon the initially good and virtuous individual, Wordsworth delineated the origins of poetic inspiration and the poet's obligation toward mankind.

To make himself, with all his virtues and shortcomings, the protagonist of a great literary work would have seemed highly improper to any writer of renown prior to Wordsworth. Most men who decided to write their autobiographies had previously established their fame with major contributions in the fields of literature, fine arts, martial arts, politics, and so on. Rousseau had founded his reputation on the publication of three exceedingly controversial works, and

Cellini's fame was based on his priceless silver and gold art works. Jung-Stilling was known throughout Germany as a skilled eye-surgeon, and Leigh Hunt could look back on a literary career of more than three decades when he decided to write his autobiography. But Wordsworth defied convention. By 1798-99 his literary achievements were still rather meager. He was anxious to produce a work which would at once confirm his poetic genius and bring him fame. Yet, he was willing to stake his literary reputation on a poetic work whose corner-stone was to be the story of his life. Just like Rousseau, he took a calculated risk, and he won. Much of Wordsworth's lasting reputation as a great poet is based on the merits of *The Prelude*.

If Rousseau had ushered in the age of introspection and *le culte du soi*, Wordsworth's autobiography provided important impulses for the autobiographical novel of the artist. Outstanding works such as Rilke's *Notebooks of Malte Laurids Brigge*, Proust's *Remembrance of Things Past,* or Joyce's *Portrait of the Artist* have emerged as milestones of this tradition in modern literature. By basing his poetic creation on the experiences of his own life, Wordsworth contributed an important subject to the existing world of fiction (both poetry and prose). But at the same time, he drove the decisive wedge into the solidly growing trunk of the autobiographical tradition, forcing any new growth in distinctly different directions. His artistic intent effected a decentralization of what had been until then the prime objective of any such work--the recording of an individual's life--and replaced it with a new one: art. To be sure, Saint Augustine had written his *Confessions* in order to show God's mercy, and Rousseau had wanted to leave to posterity a portrait of the "real" Jean-Jacques. Both works were influenced--consciously and/or subconsciously--by these desires, but the author's clearly set forth intention was to write the story of his life. Saint Augustine had experienced God's mercy and had found his destiny long before he started to write his autobiography. A desire for more comprehensive self-knowledge could also have played a role in his decision to start such an endeavour. Rousseau had proclaimed: "I am unique! I know my heart!" He knew about his virtues and his innate goodness. In both instances the writing of the autobiography reinforced already existing beliefs, but, at least in Rousseau's case, it was not expected to yield any new insights. For Wordsworth the situation was radically different.

One of Wordsworth's clearly stated objectives was his search for poetic confirmation. The completed *Prelude* would–so he hoped–attest beyond the shadow of a doubt to his poetic genius. Another objective, already pursued in the 1798-99 two-part *Prelude*, was to show Nature's formative role and regenerative powers. *The Prelude* as we have it now (the 1850 publication) embodies furthermore the poet's very definite and revolutionary new ideas about poetry and the poet's mission. Now, it appears virtually impossible to pursue with equal zeal and commitment such a multitude of objectives, especially if two–life and art–are, as we have seen in chapter one, almost mutually exclusive. Since it was Wordsworth's overwhelming desire to create a literary masterpiece that had sustained and spurred him on throughout the long and laborious years of composition, it stands to reason that the autobiographical content would be subjected to and modified according to the artistic demands of the work and not vice versa.

Again, it is not the purpose of this study to shed new light on the artistic quality of *The Prelude* or to interpret the poem anew.[1] Rather, those aspects of the work will be examined which were instrumental to the evolution of the autobiographical genre. It is an attempt to isolate those elements introduced by Wordsworth which led to new trends and developments. Thus, all remarks center on *The Prelude's* relation to the autobiographical genre, the innovations it contributes, and the changes it effects.

---

1   Some excellent studies of *The Prelude* are E. De Selincourt, *The Prelude*, revised by Helen Darbyshire, Oxford, At the Clarendon Press, 1957, W.W. Douglas, *Wordsworth: The Construction of a Personality*, Kent, Kent State University Press, 1968. H. Lindenberger, *On Wordsworth's Prelude*, Princeton, Princeton University Press, 1963. F. W. Bateson, *Wordsworth-A Re-Interpretation*, London, New York, Longman, Green and Co., 1954. R. U. Onorato, *The Character of the Poet*, Princeton, Princeton University Press, 1971. Jonathan Wordsworth, ed., *Bicentenary Wordsworth Studies*, Ithaca, Cornell University Press, 1970. Herbert Read, *Wordsworth*, New York, Jonathan Cape and Harrison Smith, 1931. G.H. Hartmann, *Wordsworth's Poetry 1787-1814*, New Haven, Yale University Press, 1964.

Before looking at the work itself, a quick glance at the date of completion of *The Prelude* yields a first clue that we are dealing with a highly unusual kind of autobiography. Contrary to all convention, Wordsworth sets out to write this work at a rather early stage of his literary career–at age twenty-eight. Although today it is not unusual to find "autobiographies" written by young people who have barely passed adolescence (actors, ball players, rock musicians, and singers) prior to 1800 the writer of an autobiography used to be at least middle aged. Cellini wrote his at age fifty-eight, Rousseau between fifty-three and fifty-eight, Goethe between sixty and eighty-two, and even Saint Augustine, at a time when life expectancy was considerably shorter, composed his work between the age of forty-three and forty-six. A man setting out to write his autobiography at age twenty-eight must have a very special reason to do so rather than to wait, assuming that each year would bring more experience and additional insights, which would enrich his work.

Very early in his literary career –as early as 1795– Wordsworth contemplated the writing of a long poem. During many a mutually enriching discussion with Coleridge, the project ripened. It was to be a philosophical poem "containing views of man, Nature, and Society," entitled *The Prelude*. Wordsworth first mentions it in a letter to James Tobin, on March 6, 1798:

> I have written 1300 lines of a poem in which I contrive to convey most of the knowledge of which I am possessed. My object is to give pictures of Nature, Man, & Society. Indeed I know not any thing which will not come within the scope of my plan.[2]

Although *The Recluse* was constantly on the author's mind and Coleridge never ceased urging him on, Wordsworth started extensive work only after he and Dorothy had settled in Grasmere in late 1799. Having completed the first Book of *The Recluse*, "Home at Grasmere," the poet seemed to hesitate, uncertain how to pursue his philosophi-

---

2   This letter precedes the one Wm. Minto indicates as being the first one to mention the project. That letter was dated March 11, 1798 and addressed to Mr. Losh: "I have been tolerably industrious within the last few weeks. I have written 1300 lines of a poem which I hope to make of considerable utility," quoted in A.W. Thomson, ed., *Wordsworth's Mind and Art*, New York, Barnes and Noble, Inc., 1970.

cal/poetical endeavour. Although he knew what he was going to write about, the structure of the work itself eluded him. In addition, he started to have serious doubts as to his capability for executing such a monumental work. In 1800, rather than continuing with *The Recluse*, Wordsworth prepared another edition of the *Lyrical Ballads,* adding his famous Preface. Indeed, after some revisions on "The Ruined Cottage," he seems to have abandoned *The Recluse* altogether. A letter written almost five years later to Sir George Beaumont suggests why:

> I began to work [on *The Prelude*] because I was unprepared to treat a more arduous subject, and diffident of my own powers. Here, at least, I hoped that to a certain degree I should be sure of succeeding, as I had nothing to do but describe what I had felt and thought; therefore could not easily be bewildered.[3]

Like Montaigne, Wordsworth tells us in very plain language: I know myself best, therefore I write about myself. This does not mean that he has abandoned his initial intention to write a philosophical poem. Not at all. It merely means that he will use his own life and experiences as the basis for this work.[4]

Wordsworth had never written a long poem, philosophical or meditative, and trying to mold lofty philosophical ideas and ideals into a poetically sound and coherent structure requires not only genius, but also a certain amount of experience. And he was aiming high. In a letter to John Wilson that falls into this period of frustration and soul searching, he sums up his ulterior motives for writing poetry:

> . . . you have given me praise for having reflected faithfully in my Poems the feelings of human nature. I should fain hope that I have done so. But a great Poet ought to do more than this: he ought, to a certain degree, to rectify men's feelings, to give them new compositions of feelings, to render their feelings more sane, pure, and permanent, in short, more consonant to nature, that is, to eternal nature, and the great moving spirit of things. He ought to travel before men occasionally as well as at their sides.[5]

3   E. De Selincourt, *op. cit.,* p. 439.
4   It might well be that it was this decision that brought Wordsworth frequent accusations of excessive egotism.
5   De Selincourt, *op. cit.,* p. 296 (the letter is dated June 1802).

These are lofty goals. And Wordsworth intended to be a great Poet, not just a poet. We must keep his concept of poetic mission as he outlined it above in mind when we examine *The Prelude*. If indeed Wordsworth did pursue these objectives in writing his autobiography (and we shall examine later on whether he did or not), he had to effect a further shift of emphasis. His artistic intentions, i.e., his desire to write a great epic poem, had already displaced the autobiographical content from its traditionally held central position of importance. Conceived and executed with the above thoughts on poetic mission, the work would also have to be consonant with the poet's didactic intentions. The autobiographical content, foremost in importance in any conventional type autobiography, would then have to be relegated to third place.

Both Dorothy's *Journal* and many of her and William's letters of this period afford considerable insight into the poet's struggles and mental agonies. As late as November 13, 1803, Dorothy wrote to her dearest friend, Catherine Clarkson, that "William has not yet done anything of importance at his great work."[6] She was still talking about *The Recluse* here, for until that time, William had apparently given no thought to any work other than the "Poem of epic length" and "great utility." But the years of soul searching and indecision came to fruition. Only three months later (February 13, 1804) she informed the same friend:

> William, which is the best news I can tell you, is chearfully (sic) engaged in composition, and goes on with great rapidity. He is writing the poem on his own early life which is to be an appendix to *The Recluse*.[7]

Impatient with his inability to proceed, Wordsworth had decided to write on his own life. Already, while in Germany during the winter of 1798-99, he had composed what is now called the Two-Part-*Prelude*, i.e., the story of his childhood years. Once the decision had been reached to continue writing on his life, the poetic inspiration

6   De Selincourt, *op. cit.*, p. 349.
7   *Ibid.*, p. 363.

74

flowed forth in unprecedented abundance. The poet, not unlike the scientist who intuitively knows of vast underground reserves, watched with utter delight the seemingly endless abundance pouring forth after so many agonizingly futile and desperate attempts at the wrong drilling sites. The poem advanced rapidly, taking shape thematically and structurally as it grew. On March 6, 1804, Wordsworth wrote Coleridge:

> I finished five or six days ago another book of my poem amounting to 650 lines. And now I am positively arrived at the subject I spoke of in my last. When the next book is done, which I shall begin in two or three days time, I shall consider the work as finished.[8]

Though Wordsworth had not decided on the exact function of the autobiography at this time, it is exceedingly important to note that he definitely meant it to be part of his great poetical work. A year and many lines later (May 1, 1805) the poet felt compelled almost to apologize for the prodigiousness of his work:

> I turned my thoughts again to the Poem of my own life, and you will be glad to hear that I have added 300 lines to it in the course of last week. Two books more will conclude it. . . . It will be no less than 9,000 lines –not hundred but thousand lines long,–an alarming length.[9]

He had accomplished part of his monumental goal (i.e., the writing of a poem of epic length about "Nature, Man, and Society,") in describing the growth of a poet's mind, his mind. Although Wordsworth realized that a poem of this length on one's own life was unprecedented in English literature, the concluding lines of *The Prelude* have quite an optimistic ring. We have witnessed his frustration and inability to proceed with his great work, *The Recluse*. When he decided to write on his own life, it was in hopes that his poetic treatment of a subject matter he was thoroughly familiar with would dispel his self-doubts and bring him the certainty of his poetic confirmation. "We have reached the time," he says in the last book of *The Prelude*, "when we may . . . suppose our powers so far confirmed, and such / My knowledge, as to make me capable / Of building up a

8   De Selincourt, *op. cit.*, p. 364.
9   De Selincourt, *op. cit.*, p. 497.

Work that shall endure."[10]

Although Dorothy, understandably jubilant, prefaces a letter to Catherine Clarkson with: "William has finished the poem!"[11] the completed work--contrary to his expressed satisfaction in the work itself--had not dispelled her brother's self-doubts as the reader might presume from the lines quoted above.

When the poem was finally concluded it fell somewhat short of the anticipated length. But its 8484 lines (in the 1805 MS) are still quantitatively quite impressive. Neither the exact function of the autobiography within the envisioned "epic" work nor the form of the work itself had been determined from the outset. The structure seemed to have taken on more and more concrete shape in the poet's mind as the work progressed. Although Dorothy had referred to the autobiographical poem as an appendix to his major work, Wordsworth spoke to De Quincey (March 6, 1804) and to Francis Wrangham (January 1804) in detail about it.

> I have great things in meditation, but as yet I have only been doing little ones. At present I am engaged in a Poem on my own earlier life . . . My other meditated works are a Philosophical Poem, and a narrative one. . . .

> This poem will not be published these many years, and never during my lifetime, till I have finished a larger and more important work to which it is tributary.[12]

The January letter seems to indicate that Wordsworth considered the possibility of writing several independent works, while the March letter points to one great work, his "epic." But only a few days later, the function of the autobiographical work seemed definitely established when he wrote: "I am advancing rapidly in a Poetical Work which though only *introductory* to another of greater importance,

---

10 *Wordsworth--Poetical Works*, Th. Hutchinson, ed., New York, London, Oxford University Press, 1967. All references to *The Prelude* will be to that edition. In order to avoid excessive footnoting all references will be given in the text as follows: *Prel.* XIV, 307-311.

11 *Early Letters of William and Dorothy Wordsworth*, E. De Selincourt, ed., Oxford, At the Clarendon Press, 1935, p. 490.

12 De Selincourt, *op. cit.*, p. 370.

will I hope be found not destitute of Interest."[13]

The *Prelude* itself and many of Wordsworth's letters indicate that the autobiography was written in search of his poetic confirmation. But when he reread the completed work, far from feeling the confidence he had hoped for, he felt dejected on many accounts.[14] In a letter to Sir George Beaumont we sense a tremendous letdown:

> I have the pleasure to say that I finished my poem about a fortnight ago. I had looked forward to the day as a most happy one; and I was indeed grateful to God for giving me life to complete the work, such as it is; but it was not a happy day for me; I was dejected on many accounts; when I looked back upon the performance it seemed to have a dead weight about it, the reality so far short of the expectation; it was the first long labor that I had finished, and the doubt whether I should ever live to write *The Recluse*, and the sense which I had of this poem being so far below what I seemed capable of executing, depressed me much. . . .[15]

A letdown and general dissatisfaction after an event that was, perhaps, too eagerly, too ardently anticipated are not uncommon. In Wordsworth's case, seventeen months of intense concentration and hard work preceded the completion of *The Prelude*. His dejection was undoubtedly intensified first by the tragic loss of his brother John, whom the poet loved dearly and whose opinion of the completed work would have meant more to him than anybody else's—with the possible exception of Coleridge. But Coleridge was not there either. The return of this cherished friend was being postponed month after month without Wordsworth's having even the faintest notion, if, when, and how his friend would or even could come back to England during these war-troubled times. Since the poem had been dedicated to him and since Coleridge had played such an important part in the conception of the gigantic work and had encouraged Wordsworth incessantly, this uncertainty must have weighed very heavily upon Wordsworth. Coleridge's reaction to the completed work would surely have been of the utmost importance to Wordsworth's own reaction. Yet, no matter how great the disappointment

13 De Selincourt, *op. cit.*, p. 371.
14 *Ibid.*, p. 372.
15 *Ibid.*, p. 497.

and dejection, it was not intense enough to make him abandon the idea of the bigger work. In the same letter to Sir George Beaumont the poet continues: "This work may be considered as a sort of Portico to *The Recluse*, part of the same building, which I hope to be able, ere long, to begin with in earnest . . ."[16]

Considering the very ambitious and very complex intentions and motives the poet had when he set out to write his autobiography and the highly emotional personal setbacks he suffered while composing the work, it is not surprising to see him dissatisfied on some accounts. While the conventional autobiography is in every instance an end in itself, his autobiography was to be proving ground and stepping stone. For other authors the writing of an autobiography represented in many instances an opportunity to review the trials and struggles that marked their way toward self-knowledge, sagacity, success, or tranquility. They had achieved by other means (whether in the field of art, science, politics, etc.) what Wordsworth was hoping to achieve with his great work. Consequently, their commitment to the writing of their autobiography was in most instances minimal in comparison with Wordsworth's all-encompassing fervor. Cellini's autobiography remained unfinished, as did Grillparzer's, Goethe's, Stendhal's and countless others'. We have seen it in Rousseau's and shall later on look at Goethe's autobiography, both of these show in their latter parts considerable neglect or degeneration of artistic quality. Goethe very obviously had lost interest in the work, and Rousseau, too worried about his enemies' plotting and his possible premature death, wrote the second part of his *Confessions* in considerable haste with complete disregard for artistic quality. But with *The Prelude* we have, indeed, come a long way from the writing of conventional autobiography, whose simple purpose had been expanded to a complex net of intentions and goals. First, it was intended to be a literary masterpiece. Secondly, as such it had to conform to the poet's very lofty and idealistic concepts of the didactic and revelatory role and purpose of poetry. Thirdly, as the "Portico" the poem had to remain subservient thematically as well as structurally to his "great work." Considering the ambitious complexity of Wordsworth's intentions,

16   De Selincourt, *op. cit.*, p. 497.

dissatisfaction with one or the other element seems almost inevitable.

In an effort to better understand Wordsworth's priority rating of his various motives and intentions, I have tried to pinpoint the source of his dejection. Since he announced that he hoped to be able to start work on *The Recluse* again, he must have been sufficiently—though maybe not completely--convinced of his poetic genius. Since he also announced at that time the introductory role *The Prelude* was to play, he must have considered it suitable for such a purpose.[17] He did not weigh down the poem with any amount of autobiographical detail (a major shortcoming in the eyes of many readers who are trying to find the man Wordsworth in his autobiography), so that we have to rule out the autobiographical content as the source of his disenchantment. By process of elimination the source of his discontent must, therefore, lie with the poetic execution or the didactic intent. "It seemed to have a dead weight about it, the reality so far short of the expectation." Wordsworth's major concern had been to write a philosophical poem that might live, a poem containing "views of Man, Nature and Society." Though he had intended to write an introduction about himself, he had--probably without realizing to what extent--incorporated "views of Man, Nature and Society." His poem--philosophical from the very start[18]--contained so much more than the poet must have intended to include. According to the above letter, he was not aware that he had said everything he had to say on the subject in his "portico."[19] Intuitively, however, as a poet he felt "the dead weight about it," an expansiveness and completeness to-

17 In the 1814 Preface to *The Excursion* the poet called it the "ante-chapel to a gothic church." Wordsworth's vision of the entire work must have been gigantic if he could view the nine-thousand-line-*Prelude* as the ante-chapel or portico, for it is traditionally the function of the portico--almost minuscule in size when compared to the entire edifice--to guide the visitor through its narrow passage or opening to the main part of the building. It is precisely by the contrast of the smallness or narrowness of the entrance way that the visitor is overwhelmed by the immensity and vastness of the nave.

18 Mr. Read disagrees with this statement: "*The Prelude*," he writes, "is not and never was claimed to be a philosophical poem" *op. cit.*, p. 34.

19 Mr. Read also made a strong case for Wordsworth's loss of poetic inspiration and sensibility, blaming it for his inability to complete *The Recluse*. Just as strong a case could be made that Wordsworth had said everything in *The Prelude*, but failed to realize and acknowledge it.

tally unsuited for a "portico." His is the dejection of the artist who has conceived the elaborate structure and interrelationships of a projected complex work and who, after having completed the first part, realizes that somehow it does not coincide with his overall anticipation and expectations.

As time went on, Wordsworth's doubts and dissatisfactions with *The Prelude* must have waned. Coleridge's exuberant reaction to the poem when he finally returned to England in 1806 is well known. Although Wordsworth trimmed the work down from 8484 to 7882 lines (1850 edition), no *major* ideas were changed or omitted, no new ones added during the forty-five years that the poet lived after completing the work.[20] The initial exuberance, however, the feeling of poetic inspiration pouring forth almost *malgré lui* in seemingly inexhaustible bounty, traces of which can be felt throughout Dorothy's *Journals* as well as in William's and Dorothy's letters during the composition of the poem, seemed to subside. Coleridge's enthusiasm for *The Prelude* and Wordsworth's often stated commitment to the great work, spurred the poet on. He wrote *The Excursion* and published it in 1814, but it fell short of everyone's expectations, containing in essence mainly reiterations and elaboration of the themes dealt with in *The Prelude.*[21] *The Recluse*, fond hope and dream of immortality, became the ghost of what William Minto calls "Wordsworth's great Failure," haunting and tormenting the poet for the rest of his otherwise peaceful and tranquil life.[22]

20 Many critics will disagree with this statement. A strong case has been made especially for Wordsworth's changing attitude toward Christianity as reflected in these changes. Personally, I believe that most changes improved the artistic quality of his work, without being sufficient proof of ideological changes. Cf. E. De Selincourt: "The revised *Prelude* represents another, less independent creed. The position into which he had now withdrawn was not for him a false position. He was sincere, now as ever. But if he was conscious of changes, as it is abundantly clear that he was, he would surely have done better to leave as it stood what he had first written for Coleridge . . . instead of disguising his former faith: (Introduction to *The Prelude, op. cit.*, pp. XVI-XXXIX.

21 See also Judson Stanley Lyon, *The Excursion: A Study*, New Haven, Yale University Press, 1970

22 William Minto, "Wordsworth's Great Failure" in *Wordsworth's Mind and*

80

In the preceding pages I have tried to show that Wordsworth's primary considerations for writing his autobiography were of an artistic nature. Since poetry and the Poet played such an important role in the conception and execution of *The Prelude*, it is not surprising that the work developed according to Wordsworth's aesthetic principles of poetry. Already in 1800 he had advised the reader in his Preface to the *Lyrical Ballads* that if the views with which his poems were composed were realized "a class of poetry would be produced, well adapted to interest mankind permanently and not unimportant in the quality, and in the multiplicity of its moral relations."[23]

Poetry had been written for centuries with didactic purposes, of course, but many other ideas expressed in the Preface were being formulated in England for the first time. Wordsworth's principal objective was "to choose incidents and situations from common life, and to relate or describe them, throughout, as far as was possible in a selection of languages really used by men, and, at the same time, to throw over them a certain colouring of imagination, whereby ordinary things should be presented to the mind in an unusual aspect.[24] Humble persons (the beggar, the leech-gatherer, the poor shepherd, etc.) and rustic life, chosen for their natural feelings and simple utterings, are at once more elemental and more genuine. In regard to the poetry itself, Wordsworth asserts that "all good poetry is the spontaneous overflow of powerful feelings" written after long and deep thinking by a man "of more than usual organic sensibility." Not only does Wordsworth explain his choice of subjects, justify his language and diction, but he candidly admits that his work is an effort to counteract the combined forces of progress and civilization, which "blunt the discriminating forces of the mind, and unfitting it for all voluntary exertion, reduce it to a state of almost savage torpor." Although the modern reader may quietly smile at such a dire assessment of the 1800's, his present position enables him to evaluate Wordsworth's message of doom on a long-range basis as well as to judge the effectiveness of the poet's proposed countermeasures. His intentions were sincere, his efforts prodigious, and since this part of

Art, A.W. Thomson, ed.; New York, Barnes and Noble, Inc., 1970.
23 Th. Hutchinson, *Wordsworth–Poetical Works, op. cit.*, p. 734.
24 Ibid, p. 734.

the Preface is judged to be of considerable importance for the understanding of *The Prelude*, it is quoted here at length:

> A sense of false modesty shall not prevent me from asserting, that the Reader's attention is pointed to this mark of distinction, far less for the sake of these particular Poems than from the general importance of the subject. The subject is indeed important! For the human mind is capable of being excited without the application of gross and violent stimulants; and he must have a very faint perception of its beauty and dignity who does not know this, and who does not further know, that one being is elevated above another, in proportion as he possesses this capability. It has therefore appeared to me, that to endeavour to produce or enlarge this capability is one of the best services in which, at any period, a Writer can be engaged. . .[25]

> . . . I have said that poetry is the spontaneous overflow of powerful feelings: it takes its origins from emotions recollected in tranquillity: the emotion is contemplated till, by a species of reaction, the tranquillity gradually disappears, and an emotion, kindred to that which was before the subject of contemplation, is gradually produced, and does itself actually exist in the mind. In this mood successful composition generally begins and in a mood similar to this is carried on; but the emotion, of whatever kind, and in whatever degree, from various causes, is qualified by various pleasures, so that in decribing any passions whatsoever, which are voluntarily described, the mind will, upon the whole, be in a state of enjoyment.

> If Nature be thus cautions to preserve in a state of enjoyment a being so employed, the Poet ought to profit by the lesson held forth to him, and ought especially to take care, that, whatever passions he communicates to his Reader, those passions, if his Reader's mind be sound and vigorous, should always be accompanied with an overbalance of pleasure. . . .[26]

This is Wordsworth's manifesto. Its principles are not just meant for the *Lyrical Ballads*, but are applicable to his entire literary production as well as to his way of life.[27] As a missionary poet, Words-

---

25 Hutchinson, *op. cit.*, p. 735.
26 Ibid, p. 740.
27 For a thorough study outlining the differences among the various Prefaces see W.J.B. Owen, *Wordsworth as Critic*, Toronto, University of Toronto Press, 1969.

worth aims to "rectify" man's feelings, to give them "new composition of feeling," to render his feeling, "more sane, pure, and permanent, and more consonant with nature and the great moving spirit." The ultimate goal, of course, is the attainment of greater perfection and therefore of a more profound individual happiness for mankind. Helen Darbishire points out that Wordsworth was "possessed of the idea of the necessary movement of mankind toward perfection."[28] Again, this goal is not an entirely new one. The eighteenth century with its frantic pursuit of "moral grace" (Shaftesbury), "*die schöne Seele*" (Goethe and Schiller), and *beauté* (by a variety of French writers)[29] strove for nothing less than man's greater happiness, and it was the poet's role to guide him thither. But contrary to most writers of the Enlightenment, Wordsworth saw the means to such an end not in reason and the achievements of civilization, but rather in the genuine and profound emotions evoked by natural environment, untouched and unspoiled by progress and science.[30] The rustic man's

28 Helen Darbishire, "Wordsworth's Belief in the Doctrine of Necessity," *Review English Studies,* Vol. XXIV, 1948, pp. 121-125.
29 cf. Hélène Sanko, *La Question du Beau dans la presse periodique française,* unpublished dissertation, Case Western Reserve University, Cleveland, 1971. Hélène Sanko writes: "L'impression générale que nous avons eue en lisant les journaux est que l'objectif final de la perception du Beau est le bonheur. Être capable de sentir le Beau rend l'homme heureux, par conséquent il faut travailler à developer son goût et lui apprendre à percevoir le beau." p. 259.
30 Similar thoughts had already been expressed in Germany by Johann G. Hamann (1730-1788) in his "The Philosopher's Crusade" (1762): "Poetry is the mother tongue of the human race. . . . They [our forefathers] opened their mouth—to utter aphorisms" as well as by J.G. Herder (1744-1803) in his "Treatise about the Origin of Language" (1770) in which he speaks out for a return to primal conditions: "The natural language of all beings, by reason translated into sound, is a dictionary of the soul, a perpetual creation of fables full of passion and interest; that is what language was in its beginning. And what else is poetry?" Glaser, Lehmann, and Lubos, *Wege der Deutschen Literatur*, Frankfurt, M., Verlag Ullstein G.M.B.H., 1961. Wordsworth may or may not have been familiar with these and similar ideas. His stay in Germany combined with Coleridge's intensive study of German Philology and the German literary tradition seem to account for some similarities in his critical writings with certain German contemporaries.

impassioned discourse emanating from immediate events or experiences are in striking contrast to the eighteenth century poet's effort to recreate situations and/or emotions with the language and diction prescribed and regulated by classical poetic guidelines.

If Gibbon could boast that he wrote "the narrative" of his life for his own amusement and that this represented his sole reward,[31] Wordsworth had taken upon himself the more serious and exalted commitment of what he conceived to be the poet's mission. Addressing Coleridge, he proclaims:

> Prophets of Nature, we to them will speak / A lasting inspiration, sanctified / By reason, blest by faith; what we have loved / Others will love, and we will teach them how; / Instruct them how the mind of man becomes / A thousand times more beautiful than the earth / On which he dwells, above this frame of things / (which, 'mid all revolution in the hopes and fears of men, doth still remain unchanged) / In beauty exalted, as it is itself / Of quality and fabric more divine. (*Prel.* Bk. XIV, 444-454)[32]

The first of the missionary's manifold tasks was his crusade against the public's "degrading thirst after outrageous stimulation." Considering the widespread opposition to the subdued and serene quality of his poetry and his choice of subjects, this was not an easy undertaking, and in the end the efforts were crowned with very

---

31 Edward Gibbon, *Memoirs of My Life*, ed. G.A. Bonnard, New York, Funk & Wagnalls, 1969, p. 1.
32 In his Preface to the second edition of the *Lyrical Ballads*, Wordsworth had outlined the role of the poet and the poetry: "The man of science seeks truth as a remote and unknown benefactor; he cherishes and loves it in his solitude: the Poet, singing a song in which all human beings join with him, rejoices in the presence of truth as our visible friend and hourly companion. Poetry is the breath and finer spirit of all knowledge. . . . He [the Poet] is the rock of defence for human nature; an upholder and preserver, carrying everywhere with him relationship and love . . . the Poet binds together by passion and knowledge the vast empire of human society, as it is spread over the whole earth, and over all time. The objects of the Poet's thoughts are everywhere; though the eyes and senses of man are, it is true, his favorite guides. . . . Poetry is the first and last of all knowledge–it is as immortal as the heart of man." Hutchinson, *op. cit.*, p. 738.

modest success. But the Preface had been conceived and written for just this purpose. The large majority of the public, however, preferred the "gaudiness and insane phraseology of many modern writers,"[33] the instant noise and excitement arising from "outrageous stimulation" to the pursuit and lasting enjoyment of sublime but tranquil happiness. The prophet's voice was heard and heeded only by a few, but his message still lives and will be taken to heart as long as there is one individual who believes in the perfectability not of mankind as a whole, but of the individual. For the grandiose dreams of the great thinkers of the 1800's who envisioned a permanently wise and happy human race in a peaceful, paradisiac world, were quickly dispelled by the harsh realities of the nineteenth century.

When Wordsworth wrote his famous Preface, he was actively engaged with the composition of *The Prelude*. While much of the Preface is intended to make the new material, the new approach palatable to the reader, the writer developed his autobiography according to the same aesthetic principles. In it the joys of the simple life, the endless delights provided by nature are underlined, and the vices and hypocrisy, the ceaseless tumult and basic corruptions of the city (London) provide a striking contrast to such an idyllic existence. It is not formal schooling that provides man with the keenest insights and greatest consciousness, nor does intensive social or political engagement guarantee long-lasting satisfaction. Again, it is nature in all its simplicity and all its complexity which, in the end, yields the secrets of all existence and thus becomes the only guarantor for human happiness. In this respect *The Prelude* is the romance-quest par excellence, the hero in search of his identity. The prophet (in this instance identical with the writer) is showing mankind how truth and knowledge can be found and happiness attained. The hero, young and inexperienced, goes through a series of apocalyptic events both pleasant and painful, in order to emerge a wiser, more tolerant, and harmonious human being. We have witnessed this development from the *Parzival Epic* trough *Wilhelm Meister*. But while the hero of these works found life's fulfillment and purpose in the ethically and

33   Paul Zall, ed., *Literary Criticism of William Wordsworth*, Lincoln, University Press of Nebraska, 1966, p. 40.

morally controlled and active interaction with man and society, the protagonist of *The Prelude* found his in the solitary, intimate intercourse with Nature.

The decision to try himself in the autobiographical vein was a very fortunate one for Wordsworth, for it seems to have had upon him an effect similar to the religious confession of a priest.[34] It removed any inhibitions and mental blocks that may have hampered poetic creation and revitalized his imagination. "One end at least hath been attained; my mind has been revived," he tells Coleridge in *The Prelude* (Bk. I, 636). Yet, while poetic inspiration flowed unhampered and the autobiography took shape, Wordsworth never lost sight of his initial objectives, the artistic and prophetic one. Meticulously he built its delicate framework, weaving expertly his physical and mental growth into its elaborately evolving structure. Contrary to an autobiographer like Rousseau or Jung-Stilling, who includes at random any event or experience he can recall, the writer of a philosophical-poetic work must carefully select extraordinary experiences or "spots of time" pertinent to the artistic development of his theme and structure. This is precisely why we look in vain for events in *The Prelude* which—at least in our eyes—would seem important enough to have been included in an autobiography, especially in view of the writer's assurance that "the discipline / And consummation of a Poet's mind, / In everything that stood most prominent, / have faithfully been pictured . . ." (*Prel.* XIV, 303-306).

In the following pages I shall examine several events of "crucial" importance in Wordsworth's life that he chose to omit from his autobiography. Why did he omit them? Was he like one of those "falsely sincere" Rousseau had had in mind? Was it a case of bad memory? I don't believe so. After a thorough examination of *The Prelude* and a careful scrutiny of the chronological sequence of the omitted events, I have come to the conclusion that it was Wordsworth's preoccupation with thematic unity which determined inclusion or omission of any given experience. G. Fernandez, in an effort to prove that

34 "Confession is a matter of directly touching the conscience, more profoundly than at any other time, and of purifying the mind more completely and more deeply." A. Snoeck, S.J., *Confession and Pastoral Psychology*, Westminster, The Newman Press, 1961, p. 5.

no analogical relations exist between autobiography and art, points out that the consciousness of the self and the work of art are two distinct realities that may borrow from each other, but nevertheless lead to independent synthesis. "The artist," he writes, "renounces the man."[35] The erratic and often chaotic realities of life seem to be in direct conflict with the single most important principle underlying any work of art: that of harmony and order. Since Wordsworth wanted to write a literary work and since this work was destined to serve mankind as a reliable and permanent guide to happiness, he had to subject his autobiographical data to his primary and secondary purpose. It is precisely this restructuring of priorities which marks Wordsworth's greatest contribution to the evolution of the autobiographical genre. Yet, at the same time, it poses its greatest threat. For how many important events, how much suffering or delirious happiness can an autobiographer omit? How many "justifying purposes" can he serve, without destroying or at least distorting the very life he has set out to describe? Wordsworth expressed his opinion on this matter in an open "Letter to a friend of Robert Burns" (1816):

> . . . you will probably agree with me in opinion that biography, though differing in some essentials from works of fiction, is nevertheless, like them, an art–an art, the laws of which are determined by the imperfections of our nature, and the constitution of society. Truth is not here, as in the sciences, and in natural philosphy, to be sought without scruple, and promulgated for its own sake, upon the mere chance of its being serviceable; but only for obviously justifying purposes, moral and intellectual.

He is particularly emphatic when it comes to the biographies of poets:

> Our business is with their books,–to understand and to enjoy them. And, of poets more especially, it is true that, if their works be good, they contain within themselves all that is necessary to their being comprehended and relished. . . . I should dread to disfigure the beautiful ideal of the memories of those illustrious persons [Greek and Roman poets] with incongruous features, and to sully the imaginative purity of their classical works with gross and trivial recollections. The least weighty objections

---

35 G. Fernandez, *L'autobiographie et le roman*, Paris, Messages, 1926, p. 45.

to heterogeneous details is that they are mainly superfluous, and therefore an incumbrance.[36]

There are certain events in each man's life—"heterogeneous details"—which decisively influence his mode of thinking, his way of life, his very future. A parent's death, a passionate love affair, marriage, and the birth of a first child, these are probably the most significant and memorable experiences in any man's life. Because of their intense emotional impact, he is not likely to ever forget them.

"Six changeful years," Wordsworth tells his readers, lie between the beginning of *The Prelude* and the beginning of Book VII. Important events, never mentioned in the work, precede these years and mark them. But the reader looks in vain for the poet's youthful love affair in Blois, France, with Marie Ann Valon in 1791, probably the single most important event in Wordsworth's life.[37] Neither does the reader find any mention of the poet's return to France in 1802 and his visit at Calais with Marie Ann and their daughter Caroline, who by then was ten years old. His marriage to Mary Hutchinson, an old friend from a respectable family, should have inspired the poet to a song of jubilation. Again, the birth of their son John in 1803 and their daughter Dora in 1804 should have been ample cause to permit an ever-so-slight digression from his intended course in *The Prelude*. Every one of these highly emotional historical experiences should have deeply affected a man "of more than usual organic sensibility." And yet Wordsworth remained silent.

For quite obvious reasons the silence in regard to the poet's affair in France[38] has been examined from all sorts of interesting psychological angles: he was guilt-ridden (Read); he was embarrassed about the whole affair, having been seduced by this very erotic but brainless older French woman (Bateson); he was reserved, even secretive by nature (Lindquist).[39] Legouis deplores the poet's waywardness of

36 William Wordsworth, "A Letter to a Friend of Robert Burns," quoted in *Literary Criticism of William Wordsworth*, ed. Paul Zall, *op. cit.*, pp.188-204.
37 Prof. Read considers this the singly most important experience in the poet's life. H. Read, *op. cit.*
38 We owe this information to Prof. Harper who during WWI was engaged in research work in France and happened upon Caroline's birth certificate.
39 Wilfred H. Lindquist, *Wordsworth's Prelude as an Autobiography*, unpub-

this period; and Bishop Christopher Wordsworth, editor of his uncle's *Memoirs*, though he copiously avoids talking about the Annette-incident, prepared for his illustrious parent a quasi—apology:

> Wordsworth's condition in France was a very critical one: he was an orphan, young, inexperienced, impetuous, enthusiastic, with no friendly voice to guide him, in a foreign country, and that country, in a state of revolution, and this revolution, it must be remembered, had not only taken up arms against the monarchy and other ancient institutions, but had declared war against Christianity. The most licentious theories were propounded, all restraints were broken; libertinism was law. He was encompassed with strong temptations.[40]

Wordsworth had originally written the story of "Vaudracour and Julia" as part of Book IX in the 1805 version. This incident bears a certain resemblance to his own love story, although the roles are reversed. The unhappy lovers are mercilessly separated by social dictates, despite the birth of a child which, from a purely humane point of view, should have assured their continued and happy union. The story was never intended to involve the protagonist of *The Prelude*, and we shall see presently why this was thematically impossible. When Wordsworth published the poem in 1820, he indicated that the "tale was written as an Episode, in a work from which its length may perhaps exclude it." "But," he added, "the facts are true."[41]

According to De Selincourt, the original version of the Episode consisted of 380 lines. Added to the 585 lines of the present Book IX it must have seemed disproportionately long (965 lines as compared to 335 lines in Book XII, the shortest chapter, and 778 lines in the longest chapter, Book VI) and the poet decided to remove this part altogether.[42] It must have been formal considerations which prompted Wordsworth to remove "Vaudracour and Julia" from *The Prelude*. This decision seems especially plausible if we remember his clearly expressed feelings in regard to the completed *Prelude* ("it

  lished Master thesis, Minneapolis, University of Minnesota, 1941.

40   Quoted from H. Read, *Wordsworth, op. cit.*, p. 93.
41   Hutchinson, *Wordsworth—Poetical Works*, op. cit., p. 96.
42   Read's theory, however, makes for more exciting reading: "It is the sting of viperous remorse" which prompted the poet to be silent. "This passion and all its melancholy aftermath was the deepest experience of Wordsworth's life—the emotional complex from which all his subsequent career flows in

seemed to have a dead weight about it"). The removal of the Episode from Book IX for structural considerations, however, does not explain why the poet did not discuss or even allude to this very personal and very emotional experience in his poem. In order to justify this, we have to look at the thematic development of the work.

A satisfactory explanation for the omission of this important incident can only be found if we remember that Wordsworth's primary goal was the writing of a literary work. If we now remember that "truth" according to the poet (in a biography) "is to be sought ... only for obvious justifying purposes, moral and intellectual," we understand why the protagonist in Book IX, could not experience the passions contained in the Episode. It is one thing to steal in the course of childhood a boat for a few hours' pleasure ride, even to admit to pilfering someone else's trap, but to father a child at age 21 and to abandon the young mother two months prior to her confinement is not exactly the exemplary behavior of a prophet intent to ameliorate the condition of mankind--no matter how adverse the condition, how mitigating the circumstances might have been.[43]

Wordsworth's primary concern was structural unity and thematic development. These considerations played the decisive role in his selection of events and experiences. Describing the growth of the poet's mind, Wordsworth followed to a certain extent the classical autobiographical pattern already used by Saint Augustine. The author describes his childhood years, which were spent in a spatially and temporally defined area. Usually this includes home and family, but for Wordsworth--whose conception of mankind's happiness and fulfillment was contingent upon Nature--River, Vale and Mountains take on special meaning and are therefore given special preference. The school years expanded the spatial area and added dimension to the moral development.

> its intricacy and uncertainty. It was this experience which Wordsworth saw fit to hide--to bury in the most complete secrecy and mask it with a long-sustained hypocrisy." *op. cit.*, p. 96.

43 Rousseau, too, had kept the birth and subsequent delivery of his five children at the Foundlings Home a well-guarded secret while he worked on *Emile* and *The Social Contract*. Only after Voltaire had discovered and published the truth, did he write about them in the most non-committal and innocent way in his *Confessions*.

90

My seventeenth year was come;
And, whether from this habit rooted now
So deeply in my mind, or from excess
In the great social principle of life
Coercing all things into sympathy,
To unorganic natures were transformed
My own enjoyments; or the power of truth
Coming in revelation, did converse
With things that really are; I, at this time,
Saw blessings spread around me like a sea.
                                    (*Prel.* II, 385-395)

Finally the university and travel experiences continued to widen the horizon, adding historical perspectives and social involvement.

Following the thematic development in *The Prelude*, we notice how the protagonist's reliance on and involvement with nature decreases in direct relation to his increase in consciousness and empirical knowledge. The young man's interest and compassion are directed more and more toward the condition of man (the old soldier in Book IV and the old beggar in London, Bk. VII) and mankind, culminating in his direct involvement in the French Revolution. Thematically the protagonist's preoccupations in Book IX are no longer focused on the individual and his happiness, but on a "new dawn" for mankind. Active participation in such a momentous endeavor must--at least from a historical perspective--have seemed considerably more valorous and ennobling to the creating artist than a mere love story. For the man Wordsworth, the short-lived, passionate love affair was undoubtedly of much greater consequence than the entire French Revolution, and judging by the number of his poems which have as their subject the abandoned mother and her child, the incident left its indelible marks. In the interest of thematic unity, however, and the prophetic message of his creation, Wordsworth could not include this experience of his life, just as he could not include the ascent of Mount Snowden at the chronologically correct time if he intended to make it the culminating experience of his life. As the momentous climax of the growth of his mind, with all the apocalyptic, dynamic, and revelatory aspects that go along with it, this event could--from a purely artistic point of view--appear only at the end of the work. Cambridge, London, and the French adventure with its accompanying dreams of glory, his involvement with man and mankind, his--what he later termed--"perverted and misguided passions," had gradually but inevitably estranged the poet from nature. This estrangement, coupled with his utter disillusionment with the turn of French political events, left the poet at the absolute nadir of his existence. In his youthful innocence and inexperience he had placed his trust in mankind. For one short delirious moment he had believed that man's happiness could be secured by man and his social institutions. He had been wrong. Redemption, i.e., a return to a happy tranquil, and meaningful life and ultimate fulfillment as a creative artist could only be found in direct proportion to his return and his *épanchement* in nature, which then, in turn, confirmed him in his poetic mission. This is the *Prelude*'s theme and every incident, every experience was chosen in order to underline or to develop it.

Wordsworth set his story in a poetically and symbolically elaborate framework that allowed him to reiterate this theme and to show the effectiveness of his philosophy without becoming tedious or overly didactic. *The Prelude*, following the epic formula, opens very effectively *in medias res*. We see the liberated and exhilarated poet standing at a decisive crossroad in his life. Behind him lies the city with its deadening way of life. Caressed by a "sweet breeze of heaven," his body and mind are filled with a new sense of freedom, commitment, and the urge for creation. A corresponding breeze within, swelling to a crescendo, a veritable tempest, forcefully announces the poetic effusion about to begin. "Clothed in priestly robe," singled out for "holy services," the poet and prophet stands forth in all his glory, pouring out his soul "in measured strains, / That would not be forgotten." In such a beginning there is no room for doubts or hesitations, for "a higher power / Than Fancy gave assurance of some work / Of glory there forewith to be begun" (*Prel.* Bk. 1, 77-79) especially once the poet had decided on the theme of his "philosophic song of Truth."

Already at the very beginning, the man Wordsworth tends to disappear under the "priestly robe" and "holy services." The poet's concern very plainly is not with the trials and tribulations of the man Wordsworth, but rather with the poet and his obligations. Only here

92

and there do we get a glimpse of the man--so different from that of the poet: "Humility and modest awe themselves / Betray me, serving often for a cloak / To a more subtle selfishness (Bk. 1, 233-234). But for the greatest part of *The Prelude* "the artist, indeed, renounces the man."

> Dust as we are, the immortal spirit grows
> Like harmony in music . . . .
> . . . . .How strange that all
> The terrors, pains , and early miseries,
> Regrets, vexations, lassitudes interfused
> Within my mind, should e'er have born a part,
> And that a needful part, in making up
> The calm existence that is mine when I
> Am worthy of myself! (Bk. I, 340-350.)

Wordsworth traces the immortal spirit's growth within the context of his concept of Nature in order to show mankind how and where eternal truth, lasting happiness, and ultimate revelation could be found. The emphasis is clearly on the development of the prophetic mind and his theme and not on the man Wordsworth. Since Nature was of an all-encompassing importance to the development of his theme, there was no obvious need for the inclusion and description of parents, friends, places, and/or dates which are the basic ingredients for a conventional autobiography. This child, the future prophet, had lived its most blissful moments among mountains, vales, and lakes. Nature had also provided the growing child's most intense moments of metaphysical fear.[44]

44 The absence of parental guidance, admonishment, or even punishment reflects the attitudes espoused by J.-J. Rousseau in *Emile*. Published in 1762, it had considerable impact on contemporary society in France and abroad. Its opening sentence "Tout est bien sortant des mains de l'Auteur des choses, tout dégénère entre les mains de l'homme" sums up his natural philosophy and diatribe against progress, science, and civilization. Rousseau is primarily concerned with moral education, "les qualités du coeur," honesty, and virtue. His pedagogical premises postulate that most gratifying results can be achieved in education if the child is only given the necessary freedom to experience and thereby learn in context, with nature as its sole tutor. It should at all costs be kept away from the evil ways of society. While for Wordsworth books are of considerable importance and meaningful at any age, Rousseau rules out any beneficial influence that may be gained

Nature and a simple cottage, therefore, were the only setting necessary for the growing child's exploratory experiences. Obviously, the child at that time was oblivious to Nature's overall importance in its development. It is the narrator who puts it for the reader into its proper perspective while "recollecting" these early childhood experiences.

Another omission which has prompted much speculation was Wordsworth's failure to mention his two brothers in his autobiography. Even his sister, his lifelong companion, is only mentioned in the last books of the *Prelude*. Christopher Wordsworth, the poet's nephew , tells us:

> The influence of his one sister, Dorothy, upon his life from his childhood, was too important to be forgotten here. Her loving kindness and sweetness produced a most beneficial effect on his character.[45]

And G.M. Harper, another biographer, has this to say in reference to Wordsworth's early childhood: "Even in these earliest days William's favorite companion was his sister Dorothy, near to him in age and similar in her taste".[46] Was it an oversight? Lack of gratitude? A guilt complex for his incestuous love, as Read seems to suggest? Or, as Lindquist thinks, one aspect of his life "irrevelant to the growth of his mind"?[47] We have to rule out oversight, for Dorothy, his constant companion from 1798 on, was too much a part of his life and work to be overlooked. We also have to rule out ingratitude for she received ample tribute in Books XI and XIV, and an incestuous guilt complex presumably would have kept her out of Books XI and XIV, not only out of the first two books. Why then did Wordsworth not mention her and his brothers when he was recreating his childhood experiences? Again, the only plausible explanation is that such mentionings would not have furthered the development of his theme but would, on the contrary, have hindered or at least disrupted it. The introduction of the various family members and the child's affective

---

from books and formal education.

45 Christopher Wordsworth, *Memoirs of William Wordsworth*, Boston, Ticknor, Reed & Fields, 1851.
46 G.M. Harper, *William Wordsworth*, London, John Murray, 1929, p. 14.
47 Lindquist, *op. cit.*, p. IV. This statement is all the more surprising since the author states: "It would seem that by 'mind' Wordsworth meant the entire nervous system, the feeling as well as the reasoning or thinking faculty."

94

relationship with each of them would have hampered Wordsworth's presentation of the gradual development of emotional and spiritual ties between child and Nature. It is for these same reasons that we find in *The Prelude* a contented, carefree, at times adventurous, at times meditative youngster, who had nothing in common with that boy of "stiff, moody, and violent temper" who had "become perverse and obstinate in defying chastisement, and rather proud of it than otherwise."[48] Yet this is how Wordsworth described himself as a boy–not as the future prophet–in his *Autobiographical Memoranda*.

The poet has immortalized his wife Mary and his sister Dorothy in many beautiful poems, showing both his love and veneration for these two most cherished persons in his life. But their presence in *The Prelude* would have been in many instances gratuitous, since their intercourse was with the man who needed their love, care, and compassion and not with the poet "in priestly robes" who surefootedly marches ahead, blazing a trail for man to follow.

Other "omissions" other "errors" could be isolated and examined.[49] Each instance would point to the same underlying causes. They were not caused by a faulty memory, nor were they an attempt to deceive the readers. Rather, they were shrewdly calculated, artistic devices to underline and support Wordsworth's dual intentions: 1. to write a literary masterpiece, and 2. to deliver his redemptive message.

48 John E. Jordan, *De Quincey and Wordsworth*, Berkeley and Los Angeles, University of California Press, 1962, p. 436.
49 Prof. Bateson deplores the fact that Wordsworth never referred to notes in order to refresh his memory. "The sanctity of the unprompted memory was an article of faith which is triumphantly justified in the poems and notably in *The Prelude*." Pointing to the poet's lack of reliability in regard to names, dates, and places, and insinuating that the poet's memory only retained selective incidents and these often in a distorted or faulty way, he calls *The Prelude* "simply the longest and best of Wordsworth's Poems of Memory." This, of course, means to completely disregard Wordsworth's all-important principle of artistic intent and creativity, so frequently referred to not only in the poem itself, but in a great variety of miscellaneous writings which fall into the period of the poem's composition.
Other critics have interpreted the omissions and changes from a purely psychological point of view (Hartmann along the Jungian principles, Onorato, and before him Read, along the Freudian lines, Douglas somewhere in between).

Any experience, no matter how important to the man Wordsworth, was omitted from the work if it had no relevance to the proposed thematic development of the poem. And the thematic development, i.e., the growth of the poet's mind, had to be shown in ascending order. Such an arrangement could not accommodate emotional setbacks (as in the Annette affair) or premature revelations (as the chronologically exact ascent to Mount Snowden would have provided). Maybe--as Wordsworth told Aubrey de Vere--"much was most wisely obliterated" by the selective power of the memory. We can accept this explanation as far as the poet's childhood and even his adolescent experiences were concerned. But we cannot believe that the memory of Marie Vallon and their child had been "obliterated," especially in view of his extended visit to Calais in 1802, only two months prior to his wedding to Mary Hutchinson.

It has been said that a man describing the life he would have liked to have led, can actually become the man he is describing. The poet unfolds before the reader's eye his intellectual growth from early childhood, through formal schooling, to his intermingling with man and society. The extent of his intellectual growth is reflected in increasing awareness and greater consciousness. Step by step his consciousness expands with every incident, every experience until it encompasses the entire range of human experience. But Wordsworth, in typically romantic fashion, cannot content himself with this limited everyday consciousness. If man is part of this great universe, if man is more than mere matter, and he is to be aware of it, then there must be moments in his life when his entire being becomes conscious of and submerged in this Universal or Eternal Being. The Mount Snowden incident is Wordsworth's culminating revelatory moment.

While writing *The Prelude*, Wordsworth became the great Poet whose growth and development he was reliving but also creating. During the course of the poem, narrator and protagonist evolve from each other and in the end fuse into each other, presenting to the reader again the unified and whole personality of the Poet he had encountered at the very beginning of the work. The past has been joined to the present and the future is implicit in the work itself. "Recollective self-history, intellectual self-scrutiny, and imaginative self-creation" are no longer the completely separable entities they had been, according to Professor Spengemann.[50] The process of "imaginative self-creation" becomes apparent the very moment when the poet, by means of a selective process, removes any autobiographical element not related to his thematic development and relives his very childhood experiences exclusively in the light of a philosophical or aesthetic concept he reached only at a much later time.

The Prelude affords the reader the rare opportunity to both follow and to assist the intellectual growth of a poet and his masterpiece. The reader's assistance, of course, is of a strictly passive nature, and the initial reader was--at least for the time of composition--Coleridge and a very select group of friends. Had it not been for Wordsworth's obsession with "his work of glory," his poetic mission, and his desire to produce it at all cost for his reader, his mind might have developed--despite its "poetic predestination" and all its moral preoccupations--in a radically different direction during the almost six years of composition of the work. Considering the poet's frustrations and self-doubts before he commenced his autobiography and the fact that, according to Hutchinson, three of Wordsworth's four great creative periods fall into the time during which he composed *The Prelude*, it does not seem too far-fetched to conjecture that maybe he would never have become a truly great poet without having written his autobiography.

At the beginning of this chapter the question was asked, why a man would want to write his autobiography at the relatively early age of twenty-eight. After a thorough examination of the facts, the answer seems to be that Wordsworth really did not set out to write his autobiography, but that the subject, because of his familiarity with it, imposed itself, forced itself upon him, inspired, and finally transported and transformed him. The great changes in and the evolution of the autobiographical genre were effected primarily by the autobiographer's changing motives and objectives. *The Prelude* demonstrates this most cogently.

Wordsworth's most obvious deviation from the conventional autobiographical form and structure is his use of iambic pentameter. Though Saint Augustine's and Rousseau's works abound in

---

50 W.C. Spengemann, *op. cit.*, p. 5.

beautifully lyric effusions, the mode of expression for an autobiographer had always been prose. The structured division, on the other hand, and the *in medias res* framework with its cyclical development had already been used in a quite similar way by Saint Augustine. New, however, is the complexity of Wordsworth's intentions and objectives. The autobiographical content (events, experiences, dates, names, even emotions) is subjected first to his artistic intent and then to his didactic or moral purpose. The poet, in other words, wanted to write first of all a work that would guarantee him immortality and, secondly, he intended this work to be a message of salvation, or rather a step by step instruction of how man could, indeed, elevate himself above the great mass of mankind by developing and expanding his mind's capability in order to attain lasting happiness and ultimate fulfillment. Thirdly the poem was to serve as an introduction, a "portico" to his major work. The autobiographical content had to be subjected to each of the three purposes. Wordsworth did not fictionalize the events and experiences of his life as the modern novelist is wont to do in an autobiographical novel. Nor did he have to invent tales and experiences. His personal emotions and experiences had been varied and numerous. They completely sufficed for the development of his theme. In the interest of thematic unity and poetic structure, however, he had to omit those autobiographical elements which did not further his purpose. But, as Rousseau had pointed out, the autobiographer sins as much by omission as by invention. Reed, discussing "The Speaker of *The Prelude*", says:

> . . .the poem is plainly intended as autobiography, a circumstance that would seem to make study of it simply as "a poem" a procedure at odds with the author's own expectations.[51]

The fact, however, is that as a literary work *The Prelude* satisfies all the artistic requirements, while it falls far short of the exigencies of an autobiography. Too often the reader has the impression that the "artist has forsaken the man." The poet and creating artist proved most successful, the poet-autobiographer in his act of self-realization and self-creation blatantly violated the established norms of the traditional autobiography.

51 Mark Reed, "The Speaker of *The Prelude*,", in *Bicentenary Wordsworth Studies, op. cit.*, p. 276.

CHAPTER IV

THOMAS DE QUINCEY (1785-1859)

In the two preceding chapters, we have examined Rousseau's contribution to the autobiographical genre. We have also seen his transgressions against the conventional autobiography in the interest of his objective. Wordsworth, prompted by a whole complex of objectives, resorted to even more decisive deviations from the established norm when he wrote his *Prelude*. Though the *Prelude* had not been published, we may presume that De Quincey, having been Wordsworth's daily companion for many years, was thoroughly familiar with his friend's objectives and all aspects of his great work. Undoubtedly, he was aware of the many liberties Wordsworth had taken with his autobiographical material when he traced the growth of the poet's mind from the infant's very first sensory perception to the confirmed poet's triumphant and culminating experience of "total consciousness." De Quincey's *Confessions of an English Opium-Eater*,[1] though radically different in most respects, seems at first glance to take the same direction, both in the pursuit of more comprehensive knowledge and perception and the transgressions against the autobiographical genre.

As previously indicated, De Quincey and his work were chosen for his examination because he—perhaps quite accidentally—pushed the Romantic quest for expanded sensory experience and greater consciousness to its extreme limits. De Quincey's total consciousness manifests itself in the dreams and visions that form a substantial and important part of his work. Wordsworth had achieved his visionary moments in direct communion with Nature. De Quincey, like

1   Thomas De Quincey, *Confessions of an English Opium-Eater*, (in both the revised and the original texts), ed. Malcolm Elwin, London, Macdonald, 1956. All references are to this edition, unless otherwise indicated. To avoid excessive footnoting they will be given as follows: (*Conf.* p. #), (Rev. *Conf.* p. #), (*Susp.* p. #).

Schiller's "Apprentice at Sais," experienced the naked and horrifying truth when its veil, woven by time and space, is forcibly removed not with the apprentice's sacrilegious hand, but by the author's opium excesses. But unlike Schiller's apprentice, De Quincey survived and was able to record his experiences. Strange as these experiences appear to the average reader, the fact that they are, indeed, personal experiences warrants their inclusion in an autobiography. However, when De Quincey no longer contents himself with the mere recording of these dreams and visions, but recreates his life in the *Suspiria* and the revised *Confessions* on the basis of these experiences, he is no longer writing an autobiography, but a work of fiction.

De Quincey, according to all appearances, was not at all aware of the importance and the revolutionary nature of his contributions when he first wrote his original *Confessions* in 1821. This can best be seen in a comparison of his explicitly stated objectives in the 1821 -22, the 1845, and the 1856 versions. When Wordsworth was writing his *Prelude*, he had clearly defined objectives and he adhered to them throughout his work and later revisions. De Quincey changed his fundamentally when he wrote the sequel *Suspiria de Profundis* (in 1845) and again when he revised his *Confessions* (in 1856). By then he had come to realize that it was not so much a matter of his being an opium eater that differentiated him from other autobiographers, but that it was the nature of his visions and dreams which set his autobiography apart from all others. And since we are primarily interested in the new and unusual elements, I shall focus my examination, after some preliminary remarks, on these dreams and visions.

The first impression upon scanning De Quincey's collected works with an eye toward autobiographical materials will be one of total perplexity, for there is not one, but there are rather three such works: *The Autobiographic Sketches* (1835), the *Confessions of an English Opium-Eater* (1821-22) and the *Suspiria de Profundis* (1845).[2] While we can readily accept the *Suspiria* as the sequel to the *Confessions* (which de Quincey had written when he was thirty-six

2 Thomas De Quincey, *The Collected Writings of*, David Masson, ed., 14 Vol., Edinburgh, Adam and Charles Black, 1889. This edition only contains the 1856 Revised *Confessions*; also the *Autobiographic Sketches* are here incorporated into *Autobiography*, Vol. 1 and 2.

years old), we might question the purpose and the validity of an autobiography, following the publication of a confession. Could such an autobiography, written after the more intimately revealing pages of a confession, be anything but anticlimactic and therefore superfluous? After a close examination of the works, the answer to this rhetorical question must be an overwhelming no.[3] The *Autobiographic Sketches* neither supersede nor complement the *Confessions*. They contribute nothing of major importance. As their title indicates, they are sketches intended to fill in, to elaborate on some previously overlooked or only briefly mentioned incidents, related to family, early childhood, Oxford, and the author's German studies. While they may be of some interest to a biographer, the average reader will find them tedious, in every respect far below the literary quality of both the original *Confessions* and the *Suspiria*.

The *Confessions of an English Opium-Eater* owed its conception and execution in its original form neither to literary ambitions (as in the case of Wordsworth), nor to the compulsion of vindication through self-revelation (as with Jean-Jacques Rousseau), but, as we know today, solely and exclusively to the very prosaic need for hard cash. Had De Quincey owned adequate funds to live a most modest, yet dignified life—even though considerably below the standards expected of a man of his social and intellectual background—he would have been utterly contented. His thoughts and preoccupations, having little in common with the empirical realities with which the average human being is confronted, roamed the boundless regions of the purely intellectual.[4] His initially stated ambitions had absolutely nothing in common with the countless and diversified writings he

3   I have pointed out in chapter II, that J.-J. Rousseau—for entirely different reasons and under entirely different circumstances—continued to write autobiographical works long after the completion of his *Confessions*. But these were in every respect qualitatively comparable if not superior to the finest passages in the *Confessions*. Above all, they shed new light on the author's later state of mind, while De Quincey mostly reiterates and elaborates events already adequately covered in the previous work. His digressions are frequently so sententious and tedious and only vaguely or not at all related to the story of his life, that he risks losing the attention of his reader.

4   "De Quincey deliberately flouted the demands of practical life as impediments to his intellectual development." Malcolm Elwin, *op. cit.*, p. 32.

was forced to produce as a contributor to various periodicals in the course of his life and which, measured against his envisioned work, must have seemed trifling and inconsequential to him.

Following in the footsteps of Wordsworth (the man whom De Quincey venerated and idolized from the time he had been seventeen years old and whose friendship probably meant more to him than any other he cultivated during his long life), he entertained lofty visions of grandiose labors destined to revolutionize man's intellectual realm, to contribute to its evolution, and to add new dimensions to it.[5] But while Wordsworth succeeded in outlining his ambitious project and in completing at least one substantial segment of it (*The Prelude* and *The Excursion*), De Quincey failed to produce as much as a concrete outline or to discuss the exact purpose, means, or direction of his intentions. We cannot help but wonder whether this work ever advanced beyond the stages of ephemeral dreams and visions, an outgrowth of his metaphysical and analytical preoccupations, too subtle, too intricate, and too fleeting to permit recording in a language which consists of basically concrete and pictorial vocabulary. In any event such a system would take years to develop, while De Quincey needed the money now in 1821.[6]

---

5   In a letter to his mother De Quincey summarizes his ambitions: ". . . my ambition was--that, by a long and painful labour combining with such faculties as God had given me, I might become the intellectual benefactor of my species. I hoped and have every year hoped with better grounds that (if I should be blessed with life sufficient) I should accomplish a great revolution in the intellectual condition of the world; that I should both as one cause and as one effect of that revolution place education upon a new footing, throughout all civilized nations, was but one part of this revolution: it was also but a part . . . to be the first founder of true Philosophy: and it was no more than a part that I hoped to be the re-establisher in England (with great accessions) of Mathematics . . . " quoted by Horace A. Eaton, *Thomas De Quincey*, New York, Oxford University Press, 1936, p. 250.

6   Most of De Quincey's biographers maintain that it was that author's dire financial need that launched him on his literary career. See Horace A. Eaton, *op. cit.*, Edward Sackville-West, *Thomas De Quincey: His Life and Work*, New Haven, Yale University Press, 1936. Also Malcolm Elwin, in his Introduction to Thomas de Quincey's *Confessions of an English Opium-Eater*, *op. cit.*, and Judson S. Lyon, *Thomas De Quincey*, New York, Twayne Publishers, Inc., 1969.

As early as 1818 De Quincey considered publishing some articles in order to earn a livelihood. In 1820 he reached an agreement with Blackwood in Edinburgh to supply a series of articles. The *Confessions of an English Opium-Eater* with the rather significant subtitle: *Being An Extract from the Life of a Scholar* was published anonymously in the *London Magazine*'s September and October issues of 1821 with the initials XYZ. (Practically all of De Quincey's autobiographical writings originated in this manner. Prof. Masson calls them "fugitive contributions to magazines and other periodicals.")[7] And, ironically enough, for the rest of his long life De Quincey, the self-styled scholar and poly-histor, was to derive his meager income from his journalistic contributions on the most diverse topics to *Blackwood*'s and *Tait's Magazine,* and later to *Hogg's Weekly Instructor* in Edinburgh. The initial success of his *Confessions*, henceforth assured easy acceptance of his articles by both publishers and readers. Encouraged by the reception of his work, De Quincey continued to sign his works, autobiographical or otherwise, with "The English Opium-Eater."

The *Confessions* consist of two parts. The author had actually promised a third installment of the work. Some readers had raised serious doubts as to the veracity of the account, and this third installment was designed to disperse these doubts. But the third part never materialized. Sick, lonely, and penned up in miserable lodgings, the author was consumed by desire to return to the tranquillity and warmth of his home, to join his beloved family at Grasmere. In spite of prospects of earning more urgently needed money and of pursuing his literary career in London more successfully, he hurried back to wife and children, the comfort and intimacy of his "cottage." the reveries by the fireplace, his teapot and his laudanum decanter.[8] When the *Confessions* were published in book form in autumn 1822, i.e., almost one year later, the author merely appended an excuse, referring to his continued struggle with the opium habit as the sole deterrent to his good intentions (*Conf.* pp. 434-443).

7 David Masson, *De Quincey*, New York, AMS Press, 1968 (reprint of the 1888 London edition).
8 Already in the December issue (1821) of the *London Magazine*, De Quincey had taken issue with these allegations. "The entire Confessions," he wrote,

During the years 1834 and 1836 De Quincey contributed, among numerous other articles, some autobiographical essays to *Tait's Magazine.*[9] It was, however, twenty-four years after the initial publication of the *Confessions* that he began the serial publication in *Blackwood's Magazine* of *Suspiria de Profundis: Being a Sequel to the Confessions of an English Opium-Eater.* Again, the series was to consist of four parts, but only two were supplied. After an interval of four more years, in 1849, "The English Mail Coach," "The Vision of Sudden Death," and "Dream-Fugue" appeared in the same magazine.

Altogether De Quincey worked on his autobiographical work from his thirty-sixth through his seventy-first year. It is, however, significant that the only additions and changes were made in the experiences *preceding* his opium dreams, i.e., the revised *Confessions* from 1856 culminates just like the original version in the opium dreams which had, however, been expanded to include the *Suspiria*, and several more detailed dreams. Though quite sporadic in his literary output, De Quincey produced in the course of almost four decades a rather considerable collection of the most varied articles. As his reputation as a man of letters grew, he tried to bring some semblance of order into his great mass of writings. Since the greater part of his production--including the *Autobiographic Sketches*--lacked by its very nature cohesion and continuity, it followed that his final and lasting reputation would be built upon his first-produced major literary effort, his autobiographical work. When De Quincey prepared the publication of *Selections Grave and Gay*, he therefore focused most of his attention on these writings.[10] He opened the series with the *Autobiographic Sketches* which he supplemented with articles dating back to 1834, and he rounded them out with sections from the *Suspiria* and current contributions he was then making to *Hogg's Weekly Instructor.* However, when he later

"were designed to convey a narrative of my own experiences as an Opium-Eater, drawn up with entire simplicity and fidelity to the fact" (*Conf.* p. VII).

9   These articles were published as "Sketches of Men and Manners from the Author of the *Confessions of an English Opium-Eater.*"

10 I am greatly indebted to Professor Elwin for a better understanding of the facts surrounding the various and confusing publications, dates of revision, and rearrangement of already published materials, *op. cit.*

turned to the revision of the *Confessions* for volume five, he encountered considerable obstacles. Having used parts of the *Suspiria* for the *Autobiographic Sketches*, he felt compelled to "doctor the book, and expand it into a portliness that might countenance the price."[11] The author insisted, however, that "nothing has been added which did not belong to the outline" of the original publication in 1821.

In 1856, after having worked slavishly on the revision of the *Confessions*, De Quincey wrote to his daughter about his "enormous labor." He expressed his feeling that the work "ought to be improved," but wondered at the same time "whether many readers will not prefer it in its original fragmentary state to its present full-blown development."[12] He correctly anticipated the general reaction. Having "padded the book enough to compare favorable with the "sister volumes of 320 and 360 pages," he had removed its freshness and shapely countenance. But more detrimental to the autobiographical genre than the "padding" and its negative effects, was--as we shall presently see--the new objective with which the author had already published the *Suspiria* in 1845, and which becomes clearly visible in the revised *Confessions*.[13]

11 Letter to De Quincey's daughter quoted in Alexander Japp, *Thomas De Quincey: His Life and Writings: With Unpublished Correspondence*, London, 1890, pp. 387-388.

12 " The *Confessions* stand alone," tells us E. West, ". . . None of them [his later writings] attains the unity of the earlier work at least in its first version. They lack the concentrated intensity, the ease, the passionate fluency, which made the *Confessions* so astonishing, so eternally fresh a work of art. The reason is plain: nothing else De Quincey wrote was so immediately the outcome of personal experience--in this case, of an overwhelming one." Edward S. West, *Thomas De Quincey*, New Haven, Yale University Press, 1936, p. 170.

13 In the preceding pages I pointed to the general confusion surrounding different editions. "There are three extant editions of De Quincey's works, all of which differ from one another in what they include. The first is the American edition of Messrs. Ticknor and Fields, issued in the "fifties'; the second is the *Selections Grave and Gay*, published also in the 'fifties' by James Hogg. . . Lastly, there is the Masson edition, published by the house of Black, in 1889-90. . . . The titles of the various articles in the latter edition, as well as the arrangement of material, are substantially different from those

When the author first published his *Confessions*, he tells the reader, he drew up the "record of the remarkable period" of his life "so that it may prove useful and instructive in a considerable degree." Yet, he is not attempting to write a didactic work. Its "usefulness" would by necessity be limited to a very select group of readers, namely opium users. For the great majority of readers it must have been a choice tidbit of sensationalism (on which newspapers and periodicals thrive at all times) clad in delightful and exquisitely new prose.[14] The author tells us "The object was to display the marvellous agency of opium, whether for pleasure or for pain: if that is done - the action of the piece has closed" (*Conf.* p. 431). The real originality, his big contribution, was not his "display of the marvellous agency of opium," but rather his dreams and visions.

We have already examined Rousseau's extreme propensity for introspection and reverie. In disbelief we watched him bare his soul. We marvelled at his complete sincerity, only to find out that he adhered to it only as long as it served his purpose. If Rousseau had analyzed the darkest recesses of the soul, Wordsworth had undertaken to trace the soaring flights of the mind. We have followed the growth of his mind and witnessed the gradual expansion of his consciousness to the point where it merged with the Eternal, the Universal, the *Weltseele*. Both the conscious and the supraconscious have been explored and experienced. It was left to De Quincey to experiment and write about the subconscious. And the only way to explore this was by means of his artificially induced dreams and fantasies. He luxuriated in them, relished them, cultivated them. He abandoned himself

of De Quincey's own choice," quoted from Edward Sackville-West, *op. cit.*, p. XI. In order to avoid further confusion, I shall limit my observations to the texts presented in the Macdonald publication, which was edited by Malcolm Elwin in 1956, leaving aside the *Autobiographic Sketches*.

14 Malcolm Elwin in his Introduction to the *Confessions* points out very rightly that "for prose they [John Wilson and De Quincey] would induce the same romantic revolution as Coleridge and Wordsworth for poetry, replacing the fashion for colourless correctness and ornate pomposity instituted by Gibbon with a style virile and emotional, fluent in melody and rhythmic grace, rich in many-tinted sparkle like rippling water under a changing sky," *op. cit.*, p. 38.

to them, wallowed in them, and finally was tortured, haunted, and exasperated by them because, like the sorcerer's apprentice incapable of controlling the powers he had summoned, he feared to be engulfed and destroyed by them.

When Wordsworth set out to write *The Prelude*, he was fully aware of the novelty and the singularity of his projected work. He had clear-cut objectives and the completed work measured up to these intentions. De Quincey had only one objective: To write his *Confessions*. Though he was fully aware of the singularity of his opium experiences, he failed at the time (1821) to grasp the full extent of his monumental contributions to autobiography in the realm of the subconscious world of dreams, fantasies, visions, and deliriums. To be sure, the utilization of the dream as a literary device was as old as literature itself, but never before had the world of dreams and visions usurped the place of conscious reality in an autobiography. Sometime between the completion of the *Confessions* and the conception of the *Suspiria*, De Quincey must have become dimly aware that the dreams constituted an important element in his work. In his Introductory Notice to the *Suspiria* he writes: "The object of the work," and here he is referring back to the *Confessions*, "was to reveal something of the grandeur which belongs potentially to human dreams," and "the *Opium-Confessions* were written with some slight secondary purposes of exposing this specific power of opium upon the faculty of dreaming, but much more with the purpose of displaying the faculty itself; and the outline of the work travelled in this course" (*Susp.*, p. 447).[15]

15 Preparing the publication of his collected works in 1853, De Quincey states in the "General Preface" that he ranks the *Confessions* and the *Suspiria* "as a far higher class of composition" than his other writings. "As modes of impassioned prose ranging under no precedents that I am aware of in any literature" these two works presented some unique problems to the author. "First," he tells us, "I desire to remind him [the reader] of the perilous difficulty besieging all attempts to clothe in words the visionary scenes derived from the world of dreams, where a single false note, a single word in a wrong key, ruins the whole music; and, secondly, I desire him to consider the utter sterility of universal literature in this one department of impassioned prose; which certainly argues some singular difficulty, ... " Thomas De Quincey *The Collected Writings of . . .*, Edinburgh, Adam and Charles Black, 1889, Vol. 1, p. 14.

The author succeeded in showing the influence of opium upon "the faculty of dreaming," and the general outline of the work did travel "in this course." The potential for dreams, "the faculty itself," however — i.e., without the stimulus of opium, a natural predisposition for dreaming which in a poetically structured sequence gradually and very plausibly leads to the opium dreams — that was not shown in the original *Confessions*, but only in the *Suspiria* and the revised *Confessions*. The fact that De Quincey never *fully* grasped the portent of his dreams can best be seen in the revised Preface (1856) where, for five pages, he discusses the advantages and benefits of opium, its increased use especially among Manchester work-people, and then concludes: "what I contemplated in these Confessions was to emblazon the power of opium--not over bodily disease and pain, but" (and this seems almost parenthetical) "over the grandeur and more shadowy world of dreams" (*Conf.* rev.ed., p. 99).

In the original version of the *Confessions*, we find one casual reference to dreaming prior to the author's use of opium. After having run away from school and after his walking tour through Wales, the truant youngster found an asylum in a huge, semi-abandoned house in Greek Street, where he spent his nights in the company of a ten year old child. Racked by hunger pains and stinging cold, he tells us that "besides the tumultuousness of my dreams (which were only not so awful as those which I shall have to describe hereafter as produced by opium) my sleep was never more than what is called dog sleep" (*Conf.*, p. 363). No attempt is made to describe the nature or content of these dreams. But the author very adroitly— in an obvious attempt to maintain the reader's interest--hints at future and more "awful" experiences which he is about to narrate. If we examine the "Preliminary Confessions," i.e., his experiences preceding his opium indulgences, we find that De Quincey, like most young men, enjoyed healthy and undisturbed sleep. On one occasion --after the nightmares in London--he slept so soundly on the open mail coach that he missed his appointed stop. Even during a chilly night spent sleeping under a tree, no dream troubled his rest. There is not one single incident recorded in this part of the *Confessions* which would lead the reader to believe that the author actually had a natural predisposition for dreaming or visions. We are directly led to the opium-induced world of fantasia and dreams:

> Oh! just, subtle, and mighty opium! that to the hearts of poor and rich alike, for the wounds that will never heal, and for 'the pangs that tempt the spirit to rebel,' bringest an assuaging balm: eloquent opium! that thy potent rhetoric stealest away the purposes of wrath; and to the guilty man, for one night givest back the hopes of his youth, and hands washed pure from blood; and to the proud man, a brief oblivion for
>
> > Wrongs unredress'd, and insults unavenged;
>
> that summonest to the chancery of dreams, for the triumphs of suffering innocence, false witnesses; and confoundest perjury; and dost reverse the sentences of unrighteous judges:—thou buildest upon the bosom of darkness, out of the fantastic imagery of the brain, cities and temples, beyond the art of Phidias and Praxiteles—beyond the splendour of Babylon and Hekatompylos: and 'from the anarchy of dreaming sleep,' callest into sunny light the faces of long-buried beauties, and the blessed household countenances, cleansed from the 'dishonours of the grave.' Thou only givest these gifts to man; and thou hast the keys of Paradise, o, just, subtle, and mighty opium! (*Conf.*, p. 399)[16]

This is De Quincey's hymn to joy, the enthusiastic and unrestricted submission to his god and mistress, contained in one little receptacle. The exuberance of one who has found eternal salvation echoes in these lines, and the certitude that no one and nothing can ever take it away again. And for some thirteen years De Quincey gave himself up to the pleasures of grandiose dreams, delightful fantasies, and fleeting noon-day visions, never too sure when and where one ended and the other commenced.

Since his stated objective had been to show the "marvellous agency of opium," the preliminary confessions, i.e., the childhood and adolescent experiences leading up to the pleasures and eventually

---

16 cf. Saint Augustine: "Thou shalt light my candle, O Lord my God, Thou shalt enlighten my darkness: and of Thy fulness have we all received, for Thou art the true light that lighteth every man that cometh into the world; for in Thee there is no variableness, neither show of change." *op. cit.*, Bk. IV, p. 69.

Several passages in De Quincey's work bear striking resemblance to Saint Augustine's work in style, diction, and mood. The author, of course, was familiar with Augustine's work and praises it extensively in the *Autobiographical Sketches*.

the pains of opium, consisted of a mere 32 pages. The greatest part was devoted to the author's London experience, because he felt in later life that the physical privations he endured there were the direct cause for his delicate constitution, and therefore, for his addiction to the drug. A mere six pages are devoted to the description or rather outline of the first seventeen years of his life. Nothing unusual, nothing worth recording marks the course of these years. The only repeatedly mentioned characteristic is young De Quincey's accomplishment in Greek. It was only after years of opium abuse that numerous "extraordinary experiences" related to his childhood years evolved from the mysterious depth of the subconscious mind.

Twenty years passed before De Quincey published the *Suspiria de Profundis*. By then, he had valiantly, though unsuccessfully, fought his battles with opium. And he had come to terms with it.[17] During these years, marked by visions and dreams, the author had reached a new consciousness and a new perspective on man's existence. He had pondered the possible relationships between his opium dreams and long-forgotten incidents in his life. His new work reflects these meditations. There he comes to several conclusions: a. there are not many people in whom the faculty of dreaming splendidly is developed; b. we live in restless, tumultuous times so that "the brain is haunted as if by some jealousy of ghostly beings moving amongst us;" c. "the fierce condition of eternal hurry" in which we live our lives "is likely to defeat the grandeur which is latent in all men." De Quincey feels that it is precisely the power of dreaming which suffers most.

> The machinery for dreaming planted in the human brain was not planted for nothing. That faculty, in alliance with the mystery of darkness, is the one great tube through which man communicates with the shadowy. And the dreaming organ, in connection with the heart, the eye and the ear, compose the magnificent apparatus which forces the infinite into the chambers of a human brain and throws dark reflections from eternities below all life upon the mirrors of that mysterious camera obscura—the

17 De Quincey accepted his defeat philosophically and without rebellion for, he tells us, "in the imagery of my dreams. . . I saw through vast avenues of gloom those towering gates of ingress which hitherto had always seemed to stand open, now at last barred against my retreat, and hung with funeral crape" (*Susp.*, p. 450).

sleeping mind. (*Susp.*, p. 448).

To bring the infinite within the reach of man, to condense milleniums of mankind's struggles, hopes, miseries, and achievements into one short dream, one fleeting vision, these are the possibilities inherent in the "machinery. . . planted in the human brain." To delight in Nofretete's beauty, be aghast at Brutus' murder, hail the victorious armies of Alexander, in one word, to relive history a thousand times over, hoping to discover its ultimate purpose and end, such are the experiences and the hopes of the opium-eater. The dream is to complement the knowledge acquired by "the heart, the eye, and the ear," It is destined to make man *allwissend* and therefore, all powerful.[18]

De Quincey in this passage is hinting at the omnipresence of infinite knowledge within each individual[19] which can be called forth at the discretion of the individual. All he has to do if his natural faculty for dreaming is not performing adequately, is to reach for a tiny dose of opium. But man is not God. His senses are limited (or as the Romantics insist: dulled), but for his very own protection. De Quincey's horrifying experiences bring this out quite clearly. Man's consciousness can be expanded only so much, before he is in danger of "losing his mind." Only a very narrow line seems to separate utmost consciousness and acutest perception from insanity. Hölderlin and Nietzsche, who wrote some of their finest works in the zones bordering abysmal darkness, are perfect examples of such a situation. When De Quincey "awoke in struggles," and cried aloud "I will sleep no more!" he realized that he had descended into the darkest depths of all ages, had been granted a look at infinity; but he realized at the same time that he had reached the very limits of his endurance. If he

18 De Quincey's preoccupation with dreams ties in with the Romantics' fascination with this phenomenon, but because of his opium experiences it takes on special significance. Wackenroder, Tieck, Novalis, and E.T.A. Hoffmann have made extensive use of the dream and the dream-world in their novels.

19 Rainer Maria Rilke was to develop a very similar idea. He perceives in man's present mental, moral, and spiritual make-up the seeds of mankind's entire history which trouble and burden modern man. cf. especially *The Notebook of Malte Laurids Brigge*.

wanted to live, if he wanted to safeguard his sanity, he had to free himself of these dreams.

The idea of the inherent "machinery for dreaming" must have appeared an ideal substratum, along whose lines the *Confessions* could be revised. In the *Suspiria* De Quincey poses already the very rhetorical question whether it was opium or opium in combination with something else that accounted for the dream experiences. Maybe it was a childhood experience, "terrific grief which I passed through," which "drove a shaft for me into the worlds of death and darkness which never again closed," and through which he "ascended and descended at will." Clearly do we see here the experienced writer at work. He knows he has his reader's attention. But the reader is already familiar with the climax of the story of his life, i.e., the opium dreams. Since they represent the non plus ultra in human experience, the author has only one alternative left in order to retain this attention; he must make skillful use of every literary convention by creating an entertaining, suspenseful, and dramatic plot. He must create a narrative of dramatic impact from "incidents that for themselves would be–less than nothing," (*Susp.*, p. 455) but which, seen through his opium dreams, have taken on new significance. Such a "childhood experience"--traumatic in its effect--could directly and inevitably lead to his opium dreams.

De Quincey does not have to search too hard. "Rarely do things perish from my memory that are worth remembering," he tells us (*Susp.*, p. 480). As in every family, a fair share of deaths are scattered across the path of his early youth. His sister Jane died in 1790, within a few months of his maternal grandmother. His father was buried in 1793, and his sister Elizabeth--two years his senior--died in 1792. Any one of these deaths would have been suitable to mark --poetically transfigured–a turning point in young De Quincey's life. Goethe uses his grandmother's demise and the changes it entailed as the great apocalyptic event in his early youth. Rousseau traces the beginning of all his calamities to the premature death of his mother; and Wordsworth feels life's cruel pangs for the first time when his father's corps was carried from the home. The death of De Quincey's father with all its ensuing changes within the household, change of residence, etc., would have logically offered itself as a traumatic experience to an eight year old boy. But then it is important to remember that De Quincey is looking for a childhood experience with "terrific grief" which left, so-to-speak, its permanent impressions on the child's mind and which would, or at least could, in part explain both the origin and substance of his opium dreams. Through most careful selection and sagacious development a well-chosen incident or two could, in fact, already contain the later opium dreams *in nuce*.

From the overall tenor of the *Confessions* the reader gathers that young De Quincey had a profound respect for both his parents but that he felt little emotional attachment to them. The father, tending to his business ventures, was absent from the house during long intervals, so that his death for the young children must have seemed not more than an extended business trip. The death of a grandmother is, by her very age, a rather natural occurence and not designed to elicit --even in a most elaborate poetic treatment--excessive amounts of pathos. The death of a young, innocent child, on the other hand, must literally impose itself for such purpose. And the author had two to choose from. He was four-and-a-half years old when his sister Jane died, he was seven when Elizabeth, "who had crowned the earth with beauty, and had opened to my thirst fountains of pure celestial love," succumbed to her illness (*Susp.*, p. 474). Inseparable though a three and four-year-old might be, their very age precludes the establishment of the same kind of relationship that exists between a seven and a nine-year-old. Furthermore a four-year-old usually lacks a thorough understanding of death. Jane had gone away and young De Quincey, in the innocence of youth "trusted that she would come again" (*Susp.* p. 461). Elizabeth's death offered therefore the best prospect to create a highly dramatic incident, so traumatic, so terrific as to engrave itself indelibly and for all times upon his conscious mind.

Every reader, in the course of his life, goes through a series of sad, tormenting, and painful experiences. We all have lost loved ones and we know the agonies of such losses. But we also know that passing time and other events will gradually numb the pain, push the vivid memories of the tormenting last moments more and more in the background, until growing dimmer and dimmer, they are, after a number of years, all but effaced. If De Quincey wants to convince his

113

reader of the lasting and tormenting effects that his sister's death had upon his psyche, he must, indeed, create an incident so uniquely different in every aspect, so intensely edifying or horrifying that it remained unparalelled by anything that happened to him in later life.

Before describing this crucial event, De Quincey, in order to heighten the dramatic impact of his traumatic experience, draws a loving picture of his sister. "Dear, noble Elizabeth, around whose ample brow, I fancy a *tiara* of light or a gleaming *aureola* in token of thy premature intellectual grandeur." The adjective "noble" conveys a very special image of a stately countenance and measured majesty. (It certainly does not apply to the average nine-year-old girl in pigtails, impatiently gnawing her lips because the second set of teeth seems to take forever filling up the empty spaces.) The "noble brow" complements the picture of a stately young lady, who with the "tiara of light gleaming" around her head ("which for its superb developments, was the astonishment of science") is raised up on a pedestal usually reserved for saints. She was not merely beautiful to behold, as a "pillar of fire" she went before her brother "to guide and to quicken." Elizabeth was not only "companion," she was "the leader" with the guiding light. When she died the "pillar of darkness did too truly shed the shadow of death over" her brother's heart. De Quincey brings here into full play his skillful use of contrasts and opposites: life-death, fire-darkness, heavenly presence-utter loneliness, the glories of dawn-the darkness of hurricane, memorable love-memorable bereavement. The imagery, the vocabulary portraying his sister is such as would describe a saint, a goddess. Her life is "blessing" for her brother, her death is utter "perdition." She was the "lamp lighted in Paradise" kindled only for him. After this resplendant portrait of Elizabeth in all of life's glory, the author now, poetically underlining the shattering impact of her death, is working toward an archetypical event, reminiscent of the days of the Old Testament.

> O! moment of darkness and delirium, when a nurse awakened me from that delusion [that dawn would soon arise after a night of trouble] and launched God's thunderbolt at my heart in the assurance that my sister must die. . . mere anarchy and confusion of mind fell upon me. Deaf and blind I was, as I reeled under the revelation. (*Susp.*, p. 464 [brackets added]).

Elemental, chaotic forces are at work, overthrowing the serene contentment that brother and sister had enjoyed. "God's thunderbolt," an incomprehensible act of violence, is sure to reach its destination and to wreak destruction. The reader can almost hear the almighty thundering command: thou shalt die! No wonder the witness to such a scene (a seven-year old boy) is utterly smitten, beyond any self-control, "deaf and blind," and "reeling." Nothing is left of the "luxury and elegance" which surrounded his childhood, "the intellectual culture" and "social distinction," nothing but the writhing elemental creature, reduced and crushed by a wrathful God.

When De Quincey returns to the narrative about his sister's death (after a two-page digression), we find the youngster tip-toeing into her bedroom in order to make his last farewell. One large window was open "through which the sun of midsummer at noonday was showering down torrents of splendour" (*Susp.*, p. 465). A greater contrast between exterior reality and the condition of the boy's inner life can hardly be imagined. Utter desolation and abysmal gloom are confronted with the brightest symbols of life, "torrents" of life-giving and life-sustaining sunrays not "pouring" or simply "shining" but "showering" down, so as not to hurt upon sudden impact, so as not to overwhelm with their abundance, but to refresh, to invigorate, to caress. Dazed by the "gorgeous sunlight," the cloudless blue sky, the boy turns and his eyes fall on the "corpse." De Quincey's choice of noun is momentarily shocking. It establishes a distinct and unsurmountable distance between the living, i.e., a feeling, spiritual creature and something rigid, cold, even horrible and forbidding. The "angel face" is still there, but the "frozen eyelids, the darkness that seemed to steal beneath them, the marble lips, the stiffening hands," reminded the boy in a most forceful way that whatever love and tenderness had existed between Elizabeth and him, had nothing in common with this "corpse."

The writer by now has adequately prepared the reader for the big moment. He has shown the sister's almost super-human characteristics, the strong emotional ties between the children, the sister's beneficial influence on the boy, and his emotional need for such guidance as she provided. The reader witnesses the shattering consequences of her death, the ultimate realization of the finality of their last meeting. All that remains to be done for the writer is to establish the decisive connection between this moment and his later opium excesses; i.e., it lends itself more "naturally" to a dramatic or traumatic culmination and has certainly greater aesthetic appeal than an upset stomach being appeased with laudanum. Three powerful images have evolved in the course of these last pages (*Susp.*, pp. 461-467): the boy's inner life, characterized by utter darkness, chaos and despair, the outer reality resplendent in midsummer day symbols of life and glory, and between the two the "corpse" of the one, who only yesterday had been an important part of this summer scenery.

> Whilst I stood, a solemn wind began to blow,–the most mournful that ear ever heard. Mournful! that is saying nothing. It was a wind that had swept the fields of mortality for a hundred centuries. Many times since, upon a summer day, when the sun is about the hottest, I have remarked the same wind arising and uttering the same hollow, solemn, Memnonian, but saintly swell: it is in this world the one sole *audible* symbol of eternity. . . .

> Instantly, when my ear caught this vast Aeolian intonation, when my eye filled with the golden fulness of life, the pomps and glory of the heavens outside, and turning when it settled upon the frost which overspread my sister's face, instantly a trance fell upon me. A vault seemed to open in the zenith of the far blue sky, a shaft which ran up forever. I, in spirit, rose as if on billows that also ran up the shaft forever; and the billows seemed to pursue the throne of God; but *that* also ran before us and fled away continually. The flight and the pursuit seemed to go on for ever and ever. Frost, gathering frost, some Sarsar wind of death, seemed to repel me. (*Susp.*, pp. 467-468)

The author has searched his past for a "childish experience" that resulted in "terrific grief" that "drove a shaft into the worlds of death and darkness." De Quincey discovered such an incident in his past and developed it poetically in such a dramatic way as to elicit the greatest possible reader reaction. His sister's death and his emotions and feelings connected with it, have been successfully transformed into an apocalyptic *spiritual* experience. With it the author laid the foundation for all future experiences of a similar nature.

But what has happened to the autobiography and to the autobiographer's creed? We have asked in Chapter Three how many experiences of crucial importance can be omitted by an autobiographer before the work loses the characteristics an autobiography must have? Now we have to ask: to what extent may an autobiographer poetically transform actual experiences without distorting his life? Already in the original *Confessions* De Quincey had pondered the fact that death seems more "affecting in summer than in any other season of the year." Wouldn't this have been the place to mention why? Certainly. And the author does indeed explain. He has three reasons: 1. "the visible heavens in summer appear far higher . . . more infinite;" the clouds are more "voluminous, massed, and accumulated in far grander and more towering piles;" 2. "the light and the appearances of the declining and setting sun are much more fitted to be types and characters of the Infinite;" 3. "(which is the main reason) the exuberant and riotous prodigality of life naturally forces the mind more powerfully upon the antagonist thought of death and the wintry sterility of the grave" (*Conf.*, p. 427). Nowhere do we find a clue that Elizabeth's death might have anything to do with such gloomy thoughts. Yet wouldn't this have been the place to at least hint at it, if her death had left such an indelible imprint on young De Quincey's soul as the reader is made to believe in the *Suspiria*? Was it really then that "the worm" in his heart, "the worm that could not die," was first planted and not, as the original *Confessions* attempts to make us believe, during De Quincey's *physical* sufferings, *his* brush with death, and Ann's disappearance in London? Or could it be that the author's obsessive preoccupation with death really dated from a much later period in his life, namely from his opium dreams? These are important questions. The answers to these questions are even more important, if we want to determine whether De Quincey's autobiography is "living up to his life," or whether the author is, indeed, recreating it through the veil of his opium dreams. If we compare, for example, the vocabulary, the images, and symbols surrounding his sister's death in the *Suspiria* with those surrounding his meditations on death in the original *Confessions*, we notice a striking resemblence. Summer day, blue sky, billowing clouds, brilliant sunshine, "riotous prodigality of life," thoughts of infinity, all these elements are already present. Only the abstract thought of death was being replaced by a real corpse. The basic elements were all there. But in the *Suspiria* the impact upon the reader is infinitely greater, because the writer has poetically transformed into a very personal and highly emotional experience what formerly had been merely a somewhat abstract reflection on life and death. The trance with its accompanying vision becomes now the dominating leitmotif for both the *Suspiria* and, as we shall later see, for the revision of the *Confessions*.

The impression of this initial trance beside his sister's death bed is being reinforced with another vision only a few pages later. The basic groundwork for such visions had been laid, so De Quincey's explanation for other such experiences sounds now quite logical: "The faculty of shaping images in the distance out of slight elements, and grouping them after the yearnings of the heart, aided by a slight defect in my eyes, grew upon me at this time" (*Susp.*, p. 474). The visions thus become "self-sustained," i.e., no stimulant such as "terrific grief" or opium is needed. All the child has to do is focus his attention on–say a cloud–and the marvelous "machinery for dreaming" will do the rest.

· When De Quincey undertakes the revision of his *Confessions* in 1856 he tells the reader: ". . . in these incidents of my early life is found the entire substratum together with the secret and underlying motive of those pompous dreams and dream-sceneries . . ."(Rev. *Conf.*, p. 113-114). This statement deviates considerably from his original explanation. Initially he had felt that his intensive preoccupation with history, "viz. the period of the Parliamentary War," his extensive readings on the greatest variety of topics, and his London experience had been the direct sources of his opium dreams. The author mentions, in fact, specific readings, actual experiences or encounters which, though enlarged, embellished, multiplied in the dreams, adequately substantiate such claims. But in the revised version it is no longer accumulated empirical knowledge stored in the background of the conscious mind which is brought to the fore with the help of opium, but on the contrary intuitive, *a priori* (to use Kant's terminology) knowledge brought forth by extraordinary circumstances. But not every person is wont to discover this facility. De Quincey tells us: "Habitually to dream magnificently, a man must have a constitutional determination to reverie" (*Susp.*, p. 447). And "there are not perhaps very many in whom it is developed" (*Ibid.*).

118

In the spirit of the tenets established with the *Suspiria*, he proceeds to revise his *Confessions*, letting the reader know that he, indeed, is one of the few.

We have previously remarked on the complete absence of any dream incidents in the original *Confessions* which might have pointed to De Quincey's predisposition for reverie, dreams, or visions. But the revised work pursues the same theme as the *Suspiria*. The author here proceeds with his poetic development very much in the same way as with the preparations for his initial vision after his sister's death. Even the vocabulary, the imagery, symbols, etc., bear a striking resemblance. The scene is set in Shrewbury. The truant youngster, after his walking tour through Wales, is London-bound. He is now seventeen years old. He has arrived on foot, a fact which in the eyes of the inn-keeper put him in a somewhat dubious light. Matters were, however, immediately put right, after he had announced his intentions to take the "night mail" to London. The young man then received all the elaborate attention due a gentleman of his social standing and education. It had been a day "of golden sunshine" which again had given rise to thoughts of death, of Infinity. "So sweet, so ghostly, in its soft, golden smiles, silent as a dream, and quiet as the dying trance of a saint, faded through all its stages this departing day" (Rev. *Conf.*, p. 225). But such feelings were quickly forgotten, once he had arrived at the inn. "Four wax-lights were carried before" him by "obedient mutes," a picture designed to conjure visions of the grandiose entrance of royalty, but also of a funeral cortege, pointing to the end, the veritable "burial," of the young man's carefree, pleasant wanderings. In a deeper sense it projects the end of the hitherto uncomplicated, well-provided-for existence of a young man of some means and a not inconsiderable amount of social decorum. Though the author insists that the waxlights were "too customary a form to confer much distinction," the following paragraph tends to counteract this assertion:

> The wax-lights, . . . moved pompously before me, as the holy, holy fire, the inextinguishable fire and its golden hearth, moved before Caesar semper Augustus, when he made his official or ceremonial *avatars*. Yet still this moved along the ordinary channels of glorification: it rolled along ancient grooves: I might say indeed, like one of the twelve Caesars when dying,

Ut puto, Deus fio (It's my private opinion that at this very moment I am turning into a God), but still the metamorphosis was not complete. *That* was accomplished when I stepped into the sumptuous room allotted to me. It was a ball-room of noble proportions, lighted, if I chose to issue orders, by three gorgeous chandeliers, not basely wrapped up in paper, but sparkling through all their thickets of cristal branches, and flashing back the soft rays of my tall waxen lights. There were, moreover, two orchestras, which money would have filled within thirty minutes. And, upon the whole, one thing only was wanting,–viz. a throne–for the completion of my apotheosis. (Rev. *Conf.*, p. 226)

Though grandiose in its setting, the entire scene projects a feeling of deception, of artificiality. The very elaborately created scenery, with the young man's accompanying flights of fantasy, seems prone to immediate collapse. There seems no need to insist that the young man, who had spent a considerable number of nights in the open, felt himself at this moment "on top of the world." To the autobiographer from the vantage point of 1856, these years filled with innocent joy and raptures, unbroken by intermittent periods of misery and suffering (for they preceded the very beginning of a period of utmost want and despair), this last night in a respectable inn must have taken on aspects of unparalleled luxury and grandeur. To have been treated as a gentleman of some means must have afforded the exceedingly class –conscious De Quincey–who would rather do without a meal than forego the customary tipping of a servant–a deep sense of satisfaction and self-esteem. Surely, he is not exaggerating when he remarks parenthetically that "at this moment," i.e., the moment he is in the process of recording these events some fifty-three years later, "I am turning into a God." Such a feeling is wholly commensurate with the vocabulary he uses: the "inextinguishable fire" and its "golden hearth," the "mutes", the lights that moved "pompously" before him "as the holy–holy fire."

Now we must stop again and ask ourselves: would or could the arrival of a seventeen year old pedestrian at an English country inn involve such a ceremony requiring special pomp and circumstance? Is there any need for the "glorification" of such a commonplace incident? Can we conceive the existence of such a "sumptuous" room within the means of such a boy at such an inn? Such an adjective would normally be reserved for a palatial residence of a Louis XIV, like Versailles, or of a Ludwig II of Bavaria, like Linderhof or Chiemsee. The ball-room size of the room and its towering height, the "three gorgeous chandeliers" with their "thickets of crystal branches" assuredly substantiate the impression that the writer--despite an explanatory and unconvincing footnote regarding this highly unusual pomp "allotted to him"--is poetically transforming an incident which, in retrospect, has taken on an aura of symbolical importance it originally never had. For some glorious moments, he owned a "kingdom" and luxuriated in its possession, before the dark forebodings in the shape of fierce winds worked a complete reversal of his exhilarated mood.

Within three hours after his arrival "the lovely weather" had undergone as drastic changes as his life was about to undergo. "Fierce winds" had come up, "and the whole atmosphere had . . . become one vast laboratory of hostile movements in all directions. Never before," he assures us, had he "consciously witnessed . . . such a chaos, such a distracting wilderness of dim sights, and of those awful 'sounds that live in darkness.' " Already apprehensive about his future in London during his walk, the town now takes on new visionary dimensions. "Now rose London--sole, dark infinite--brooding over the whole capacities of my heart," he tells his reader. And during the two remaining hours before the departure of the mail coach, while "more and more the storm outside was raving . . . endlessly growing," during this "wild, wild night" he abandons himself to visions of future terrors commensurate in their chaotic intensity with the raging storm pounding against the window panes. The "God," the "king" throning in the "sumptuous room" is instantly reduced to a lonely, frail, and anguished human being, who is experiencing the first pangs of isolation and *Lebensangst*. The size of the room which moments earlier had reminded him of festive balls, resounding with beautiful music, of his *avatar* reminiscent of a Caesar or an Augustus, inspires the frightened and apprehensive youth during the small hours of the night with horror and ominous forebodings.

The unusual dimensions of the rooms, especially their towering height, brought up continually, and obstinately, through natural links of associated feelings or images, the mighty vision of London waiting for me afar off. . . . [The] unusual altitude, and the echoing hollowness which had become the exponent of that altitude–this one terrific feature (for terrific it was in the effect), together with the crowding and evanescent images of the flying feet that so often had spread gladness through these halls on the wings of youth and hope at seasons when every room rang with music–all this, rising in tumultuous vision, whilst the dead hours of night were stealing along, all around me–household and town–sleeping, and whilst against the windows more and more the storm was raving, and to all appearance endlessly growing, threw me into the deadliest condition of nervous emotion under contradictory forces, high over which predominated horror recoiling from that unfathomed abyss in London into which I was now so wilfully precipitating myself. (Rev. *Conf.*, pp. 227 -228).

Wild was the night "beyond all description, and dark as the inside of a wolf's throat." Equally dark and frightening were the visions that such a night conjured upon a lonely youth. Even the stars, symbols of hope and consolation, "shone unusually dim and distant" when they became visible between gusts "of vapour."

Still, as I turned inwards to the echoing chambers, or outwards to the wild, wild night, I saw London expanding her visionary gates to receive me, like some dreadful mouth of Acheron. (Rev. *Conf.*, p. 228)

Again, in order to convey a picture of the young man's mental state, De Quincey relies heavily on gothic phenomena familiar to every reader, the "echoing hollowness" of huge empty rooms, the ghostly stillness of a house after midnight, the raging storms pounding against the windows. Especially remarkable is his discriminating use of adjectives, to intensify and heighten the dramatic effects of his narrative. The repetition of "holy-holy," because of its sonorous quality, conveys a picture of an officiating, incantating priest preceding the youngster like his sister's pillar of fire in the earlier incident. This is, indeed, a funeral procession. It marks the end of a carefree and unburdened youth, the author's youth.

Again, just as at his sister's death, several strong images were developed: 1. the glories of a (last) summer day, 2. the sudden change reflected in the deadly stillness, the storm "endlessly growing," and 3. his vision of London. It had been the wind which had initiated the boy's vision at his sister's deathbed, and it was the "raving storm outside" which effected now a complete reversal of the boy's exuberant, almost delirious mental attitude.[20] "Wild was it [the night] beyond all description, and dark as the "inside of a wolf's throat." Such a night is made to conjure a terrifying, a horrible foreboding of London "expanding her visionary gates" to receive the young man "like some dreadful mouth of Acheron" (Rev. *Conf.*, p. 228). The simile used evokes visions of London as a living, huge antediluvian or mythological monster lying in wait for its victims. Decidedly, De Quincey's horror of London in this passage is the direct result of the raging elements outside. And again, he who had been a living part of the serene and peaceful setting during the day, is thrown by this sudden outer change into a state of mental agony which in turn gives rise to a vision. The *Suspiria* visions had allowed him a glimpse into the realm of the dead, the suffering and infinity. This vision at Shrewbury unlocks the doors to futurity. Again, the author has poetically transformed an incident of minimal importance into a dramatic major turning point in the narrative of his life.

Again, the fact that De Quincey never mentioned his stop at Shrewbury in the original *Confessions*, while it appears of major importance to the reader in the revised work, is a clear indication that the author, after some thirty-five years on the literary scene had become extremely conscious of the heightened literary value such a treatment, i.e., such poetic transformation and elaboration of isolated events, would give to his work. Only two such events which are directly connected with dreams and visions have been examined here, which demonstrate that while creating greater suspense and reinforcing reader interest, such poetic transformation changes the character of the work in a most significant way. The practices employed by the author are more in keeping with the writing of an autobiographical novel than with an autobiography.

20 De Quincey, of course, uses wind and storm strictly as a means for greater poetic and, therefore, dramatic effects. This can best be seen in "The Pleasures of Opium" when, drawing a picture of what he considered happiness, he insists that besides a cozy cottage, "a fair tea-maker, . . . wind and rain raging audibly without" are major ingredients for such a state of bliss (Rev. *Conf.*, p. 228). At another point he tells the reader: "I put up a petition, annually, for as much snow, hail, frost, or storm of one kind or another, as the skies can possibly afford" (*Ibid.*, p. 287).

Summing up the findings of the previous examination, we see several facts emerging very clearly:

1. In the original *Confessions* De Quincey's objective is to write about the effect of opium on the faculty of dreaming. Opium dreams brought back to him "the minutest incidents of childhood . . ." which he could otherwise not have recollected. He goes even one step farther: "if I had been told of them when waking, I should not have been able to acknowledge them as parts of my past experience" (*Conf.*, p. 420). Nowhere in the narrative is there any indication of the author's predisposition for visions, dreams, and fantasies. On the contrary, he seems inclined toward very rational, logical thought and action. The only important experience during his first eighteen or nineteen years (i.e., prior to his opium experiments) is his sojourn in London and the mysterious loss of Ann(e). Throughout the original *Confessions* he considers the physical sufferings and their lasting effects on his health as the source of all future torment and agony. Of very special interest is the fact, that throughout the narrative the author attributes the subject matter (pleasant or tormenting) of his opium dreams to his multi-faceted and extensive readings and studies, as well as his personal experiences. In other words, all subject matter of his dreams is the direct result of previously acquired empirical knowledge, whether in the form of reading (history, the Bible, Livy, et al.), seeing (such strange faces as that of the Malayan, the multitudes in London, etc.) hearing (his conversations with Coleridge a propos Piranesi's plates)[21] or a whole complex of impressions (as supplied by his wanderings and the London experience). Though the dreams exaggerate, distort, amplify, and multiply these impressions a thousand times over, the author can still recognize their original source.

2. When De Quincey set out to write his *Suspiria*, his objective had markedly changed. Though announced as a continuation of the *Confessions*, it follows radically different guidelines. The author no longer shows the effect of opium on the faculty of dreaming; rather, he explores the "machinery for dreaming" planted in the human brain, that faculty which, according to De Quincey, "in alliance with

21 De Quincey, *Conf.*, p. 422–Goethe in *Dichtung und Wahrheit* admires these same plates in Book 1, published in 1813.

the mystery of darkness, is the one great tube through which man communicates with the shadowy" and which "forces the infinite into the chambers of a human brain" (*Susp.*, p. 448). Originally the opium was the agent to unlock closed doors, to bring forth from dark, subconscious depths long-forgotten incidents, to retrace them ever more forcibly upon the conscious mind, so that in the end, by the very multiplicity and vividness of these incidents, the author–at first delighted by such phenomenon–becomes horrified and panicky. In the *Suspiria* the equation is no longer opium equals dreams, but rather dreams equal knowledge of the Infinite. Thus De Quincey postulates an *a priori* knowledge of the Infinite and, though he insists that such knowledge is by no means universal, he proceeds to show his. He retraces a childhood incident of traumatic impact–i.e., his beloved sister's death–and intense spiritual suffering. While Ann(e) had been strictly related with his physical sufferings, Elizabeth's death emerges as the symbol of his spiritual agonies. And it is during these moments of intense spiritual suffering that the seven-year-old boy establishes his initial contact with "the mystery of darkness" and infinity. It was De Quincey's Mount Snowden. But while Mount Snowden represented for Wordsworth the culmination of his quest, it became for De Quincey the source from which all similar experiences emanated.

3. When De Quincey revised his *Confessions*, he must have kept the guidelines he had espoused in the *Suspiria* in mind. Early childhood experiences were worked out in much more suspenseful and dramatic detail. The inclusion and elaboration of the Shrewbury vision seemed to indicate that he would develop the revised *Confessions* along the lines of his extraordinary intuitive predisposition during childhood and early youth. But he desisted. The reason why he did not follow through is nowhere given. In view of the author's well-known revulsion for long works I venture to say, that the task appeared to him too cumbersome, too tedious. Another conjecture is that his belief in dreams equalling infinity had faltered in the meantime. As a consequence the work shows an obvious discrepancy between the author's prefatory note and the parts taken in their original version from the 1822 publication, so that in its entity the work–despite De Quincey's monumental efforts–shows less unity of form and

content than the original version.

4. The purpose of this study is not to determine if and to what extent the literary quality of the *Confessions* was improved by De Quincey's revision.[22] Nor are we interested in the psychoanalytic meaning of his dreams.[23] What we are exclusively interested in is if and how the author's dreams and visions affect the autobiographical genre. And this is exactly where the difficulty starts. De Quincey tells us in the original as well as in the revised version that "a sympathy seemed to arise between the waking and the dreaming state of the brain" and that whatever he "happened to call up and to trace by a voluntary act upon the darkness, was very apt to transfer itself" to his dreams (*Conf.*, p. 420 and Rev. *Conf.*, p. 312). Now we have to ask ourselves, what exactly were De Quincey's preoccupations in his waking state? Were they related to his knowledge acquired through his extensive studies, his actual experiences, his intuitive knowledge or—and this poses the great threat to the authenticity of his autobiography—to his opium experiences? According to the original version of his *Confessions* he had recorded his life in all sincerity. But when he transposes an incident—such as either of the two visions we have examined above—that arose from an opium dream, back into the course of his early youth, he presents to the readers a falsified record of his life. Such an account makes us, the readers, believe that the intensity of early sufferings opened for the young man avenues of communication and afforded him insights into the "world of shadows" and the "Infinite" which for the ordinary human being remain forever an unresolvable mystery. In deliberately duping the reader, the autobiographer commits a fraud. Granted, De Quincey achieved an acute state of temporal and spatial communion, he penetrated the world of shadows and death, but this happened strictly under the influence of opium and not—as we have seen—through "spiritual sufferings." The fact that neither of the two discussed incidents is mentioned in the original *Confessions* seems a clear indication that they

22 Ian Jack has done an excellent interpretation on De Quincey's *Confessions* in "De Quincey Revises His Confession" *PMLA*, LXXII, 1956, pp. 122-146.
23 Wilhelm Stekel has done the same on De Quincey's dreams in *Die Träume der Dichter*, Wiesbaden, J.F. Bergmann, 1912.

filtered through the much later opium dreams where they acquired dimensions and an importance totally disproportionate with De Quincey's actual experiences in early youth. The poetical transformations and elaborations in the *Suspiria* and the revised *Confessions* clearly relegate the incidents--and therefore the works--into the realm of autobiographical fiction.

CHAPTER V

JOHANN WOLFGANG GOETHE (1749-1831)

The changes within the autobiographical genre, respectively the utilization of the autobiography for other than its traditional objective (i.e., the recording of an individual's life), are not confined to any one particular national literature. We have observed them in French and English works, and I shall now extend my examination to a German writer. For each examination a writer had been chosen whose works, because of their widespread impact and popularity, decisively influenced his national literature. Beyond that, however, each writer, because of his widespread acceptance, contributed largely to the shaping of European literature. For example, many elements in Wordsworth's poetry and in the early works of Goethe (especially his novel *The Sorrows of Young Werther*) betray Rousseau's unmistakable influence. This is not surprising. Both men were familiar with his works. But Goethe could not have known Wordsworth's *Prelude* since it was not published until some eighteen years after the German poet's death. Yet strangely enough, the two writers violate the conventional autobiographic tradition in an almost identical manner, because their objectives were closely analogous. Goethe, like Wordsworth, considered himself a genius.[1] Though he was not looking for poetic confirmation, he was a firm believer in the poet's missionary role. He too has a message to deliver, not redemptive in nature, but destined to show the reader how an individual, making use of all the resources available to him, gradually develops every God-given human potential so that he may lead a fulfilling, harmonius life. The German poet, too, espouses his own particular views on literary

---

1   The question of "genius" predominates many a literary discussion and polemic during the late eighteenth and early nineteenth century throughout the continent. Cf. René Wellek, "De Quincey's Status in the History of Ideas," *Philological Quarterly*, XXIII, 1944, pp. 248-272.

methodology which he demonstrates and incorporates in his work. But contrary to Wordsworth, he knows and acknowledges that his objectives, when put into practice, will wreak havoc with his auto-biographical material.

It is significant that Goethe called his autobiography *Dichtung und Wahrheit* (with the subtitle *Aus meinem Leben).*[2] The title may be translated *Truth and Poetry*, as Rev. A. Morrison did for his sub-title.[3] But it was also translated *Truth and Fiction--Relating to my Life* (John Oxenford)[4] or *Poetry and Truth* (Minna S. Smith)[5] by translators more intimately acquainted with Goethe's thought and objective. It is definitely misleading to call the work *Goethe's Auto-biography* (R.O. Moon)[6] or *Autobiography of Goethe* (Oxenford's 1871 translation)[7] if *Truth and Fiction or Poetry and Truth* does not at least appear in the subtitle. Such a translation would completely disregard Goethe's frequently stated conception of the work. The poet spells out his intentions quite clearly in a letter to Zeltner, years after the completion and publication of the first three volumes (15/2/1830). He explains that the public always has certain doubts as to the veracity of such biographical efforts. It was for this reason that he indicated already in the title that his book should not be meas-ured with a scale of chronological exactitude, but should be accepted as a marriage of both artistic creation and autobiographical data.[8] He elaborated on the same thought in a discussion with Eckermann: "A

2   All references to this work will be to Johann Wolfgang von Goethe, Werke–
     Dichtung und Wahrheit, Vol. viii, Zürich, Artemis Verlags-AG., 1972. They
     will be given immediately in the text as follows (*D&W*, pt.#, p.#). The trans-
     lations are–unless otherwise indicated–my own.
3   Johann Wolfgang von Goethe, *Truth and Poetry*, tr. Rev. A. Morrison,
     London, G. Bell and Sons, 1874.
4   J.W. von Goethe *Truth and Fiction–Relating to my Life,* tr. John Oxenford,
     New York, The Anthological Society, 1901.
5   J.W. von Goethe, *Poetry and Truth*, tr. Minna S. Smith, London, G. Bell &
     Sons, 1908.
6   *Goethe's Autobiography*, tr. R.O. Moon, Bicentennial Edition, Washington,
     Washington Public Affairs Press, 1949.
7   *Autobiography of Goethe*, tr. John Oxenford, London, Bell and Daldy,
     1871.
8   Karl Viëtor, *Goethe*, Bern, A. Francke, Verlag - A.G., 1949, p. 222.

fact of our life," he tells him, "is not valid inasfar as it is factual, but inasfar as it has some meaning to it."[9] The full impact of this statement on the autobiographical genre can only be felt after an examination of one or more elaborately presented "facts" in the work itself.

Yet, despite his new approach to autobiography, Goethe felt compelled to justify his endeavour. He prefaced his work with *"einem gedichteten"* letter of a friend, who was entreating him, Goethe, to write an autobiography in order to give chronological order to a newly planned edition of his collected works. Such a work could, indeed, have given cohesion to the vast amount of his literary production, if its author had pursued such an intention. He did not. What Goethe does give to his readers is some insight into his emotional and intellectual make-up. And his various phases of development explain to a certain degree the multiplicity of his writings and his preoccupations.

Goethe's conception of an autobiography coincides--as we have seen--to a certain extent with that of Wordsworth:

> It is the main purpose of a biography to portray a man in his contemporary environment and to show to what extent it opposes or favors him, and how he formed from it for himself a point of view on mankind and the world, and how, if he is an artist, poet, or writer, he is able to exteriorize it. (*D&W*, pt. 1, p. 13).

At the time when Goethe started to write his autobiography, he was sixty years old. He had reached a point in his life and career, when a

9   On the same subject Goethe wrote a letter to King Ludwig I of Bavaria: "Diesem zu begegnen [dem Zweifel des Publikums] bekannte ich mich zu einer Art Fiktion, gewissermassen ohne Not, durch einen gewissen Widerspruchsgeist getrieben; denn es war mein ernstestes Bestreben, das eigentlich Grundwahre, das, insofern ich es einsah, in meinem Lebel obgewaltet hatte, möglichst darzustellen und auszudrücken. Wenn aber ein solches in späteren Jahren nicht möglich ist, ohne die Rückerinnerung und also die Einbildungskraft wirken zu lassen, und man also immer in den Fall kommt, gewissermassen das dichterische Vermögen auszuüben, so ist es klar, dass man mehr die Resultate und wie wir uns das Vergangene jetzt denken, als die Einzelheiten, wie sie sich damals ereigneten, aufstellen und hervorheben werden." J.W. von Goethe, *Briefe*, Karl R. Mandelkow (Hamburger Ausgabe), Hamburg, Christian Wegner Verlag, 1967, vol. iv, p. 363–brackets added.

man likes to look back and evaluate his life and accomplishments. Shortly before, he had observed in a paper entitled "The Meaning of Individuality": "The individual is lost; his memory disappears and yet it is in his own as well as in the other's interest, that it be conserved."[10] He did not think too highly of literary critics and biographers in general who, he felt, were all too often most eager to destroy a man's reputation or at least tarnish it, by dragging to the fore an individual's human weaknesses which, compared with his overall contribution, were minimal and insignificant.[11]

By 1808, the time when Goethe first started collecting the necessary materials for his work, life in Weimar had become quiet and somewhat lonely for the sexagenarian. His fame, confined primarily to the literary elite, was on the wane. The masses showed—as in Wordsworth's case—little patience and understanding for his philosophical and aesthetic concepts and preferred the novels of a Jean Paul Richter, the tales of A.T.A. Hoffmann, the plays of Kotzebue or Tieck, where the emphasis—as Wordsworth says—was on "gross and violent stimulants," on action and excitement rather than on artistic excellence and human perfection. A well written autobiography, sure to attract a substantial number of readers, would refocus attention on the aging poet and guarantee renewed public interest for a number of works being readied for publication and republication. By tracing his development, he had the opportunity to present to the reader not only his views on a variety of topics, but to show how he had reached these views. Radically different from Rousseau's motive and intentions, the goals he pursued were quite similar to those of Wordsworth. Though he was not looking for poetic confirmation, he

10 Goethe, *Werke*, vol. XII, *op. cit.*, p. 640.
11 In a letter to Zeltner (Goethe, *Briefe, op. cit.*, Vol. II, p. 417) Goethe speaks approvingly of "the monument" Zeltner had erected in honor of Foschen: "Wie übel nehmen sich gegen ein so liebevoll wieder auferwecktes Individuum jene Nekrologen aus, die, indem sie das was Gutes und Böses, durch das Leben eines bedeutenden Menschen, von der Menge gewöhnt und geklatscht worden, gleich nach seinem Verscheiden, emsig gegeneinander stellen, seine sogenannten Tugenden und Fehler mit heuchlerischer Gerechtigkeit aufstutzen und dadurch, weit schlimmer als der Tod, eine Personalität zerstören, die nur in der lebendigen Vereinigung solcher entgegengesetzten Eigenschaften gedacht werden kann."

was going to write another literary work which, like most of his writings, had a message to deliver. He was not intent on producing a masterpiece. There was no need for it for his literary fame was already well established.[12]

Goethe had been fascinated with biographies from his early youth. It was he who had encouraged Jung-Stilling to write about his life and then helped him to publish the work. He had translated Cellini's work, and in later years suggested to Alexander von Humboldt and Philipp Hackert to write their autobiographies. How strongly he felt about the value of such a work can best be seen from a letter to his friend Zeltner (Nov. 1, 1829):

> If a man wants to leave something useful to posterity it must be a confession. A man must show himself as an individual, as he sees himself. Those who come after him may pick out that which suits them best and that which may be generally valid. Much of this has been left to us by our forefathers.[13]

During his lifetime many important historical and social changes had taken place which, combined with his personal experiences, should make for interesting reading. Through an ever active interest in literature, science, and above all in people from the very young to the very old, the blushing maiden to the most renowned scientist or artist, Goethe had familiarized himself with every aspect of life and every new trend within a vast range of human endeavours. Financial independence had afforded him the leisure to pursue any studies of his choice, to follow any inclination he might feel. During the sixty years of his prodigiously rich and busy life he had pursued many of them: physics (his writings on the spectrum of light), botany (his writings on organic growth and the metamorphoses of the plants), anatomy (he discovered a hitherto unknown human jawbone), and drawing (a number of his drawings have escaped his mania for bonfires made from his works). Goethe had obtained his Licentiate in Jurisprudence at Strasburg, practiced law for a short period and later served in the capacity of Geheimrat as advisor for the Duke of Weimar. His foremost commitment, however, was and always had

12 Cf. Heinrich Meyer, *Goethe, das Leben im Werk*, Stuttgart, Hans Gunther Verlag, 1967.
13 J.W. von Goethe, *Briefe*, Vol. iv., *op. cit.*, p. 349.

been to literature. His had been a rich life, a fulfilling and fulfilled life. To write about it must have provided a deep sense of satisfaction to the aging poet, for he knew that he was, indeed, erecting his own monument.

Goethe started to collect information from family and friends, chronicles and history as early as 1808. By 1813 he had completed the first three parts. In part four he was to relate his rather delicate relationship with Lili Schönemann, his beautiful and intelligent fiancée. But Lili, now Baroness von Türckheim, was still alive in 1813 and it is possible that a feeling of continued reverence and devotion (which Goethe experienced for any lady to whom he was or had been emotionally attached) kept him from reliving and exposing this particular time of his life. In a letter to Heinrich Eichstätt (Jan. 29, 1815) the poet mentions his inability to proceed with part four without being able to explain what exactly was preventing him from completing his envisioned work.[14] Whatever the reason, the fourth and last part, in several sections vastly inferior in literary quality to the other three, was not finished until one year before the author's death (in 1831). All too often diary-like entries or long-winded character analysis, observations and tedious *Belehrungen* by the now eighty-year-old Goethe distract from the meticulously constructed unity of form and content of the preceding three parts. Since this part was only published posthumously, it is quite possible that the author had never considered it ready for publication.

Since Goethe in his title and in his letter to Ludwig I of Bavaria had clearly indicated that he took recourse "to a sort of fiction" when writing his autobiography, it seems futile to search out again all the incidents in the work which do not "seem" to coincide with historical reality.[15] We have to content ourselves with his effort to "rep-

14 "Schon seit einem halben Jahr habe ich den vierten Band, welcher ungefähr bis zur Hälfte gediehen war, plötzlich liegen lassen und, um nicht völlig zu stocken, zehen Jahre übersprungen, wo das bisher beengte und beängstigte Naturkind in seiner ganzen Losheit wieder nach Luft schnappt, im September 1786 auf der Reise nach Italien" Goethe, *Briefe*, Vol. iii, *op. cit.*, p. 292.
15 Richard Friedenthal points out numerous instances when Goethe changed historical facts "in order to present himself in a better light." While this is true in Rousseau's case, I am firmly convinced that the author, just like Wordsworth, made these changes for purely aesthetic or philosophical con-

134

resent basic truth which played an important role in his life" even though "imagination" and "capricious memory" combined with the desire to entertain and interest his readers may have enhanced a number of given events or emotions and their ensuing consequences or results. Goethe was at all times aware of and sensed the dangers of an interfering creative imagination in such an endeavour. And he acknowledged it. Totally independent of Wordsworth and in an entirely different intellectual climate from his British colleague, he made very similar use of the autobiographical data, i.e., he subjected it to his overall artistic and philosophical intent. But while Wordsworth contented himself with the omission of facts and altered occasionally the chronological sequence of events, Goethe recreated his childhood experience—as we shall see—not by relying on his deficient memory related to these days, but by diligent perusal of available primary source materials. He created a milieu which, he felt, decisively furthered his development, and he placed the child Goethe in it. In Goethe's as well as in Wordsworth's instance, artistic considerations far outweigh those of absolute and detailed historical veracity.

Again some of the more remarkable passages from *Dichtung und Wahrheit* were chosen in order to show how Goethe, grossly violating the conventional autobiography, achieved maximum artistic results by combining factual autobiographical detail with imaginative, artistic talent, how the poet used literary conventions to achieve maximum suspense and elicit the reader's interest from often insignificant and trivial autobiographical detail. But first a very short and very general resume of the work will be given, since *Dichtung und Wahrheit*, unlike Rousseau's *Confessions* and Wordsworth's *Prelude*, is not too well known in the English speaking world.

The external structure of Goethe's autobiographical work is divided into four parts, each consisting of five books. I have previously pointed to the deficiency and obvious incompleteness of part four.

considerations. (Cf. *Goethe: His Life and Times*, Cleveland, The World Publishing Co., 1963). E.R. Beutler, studying the inconsistencies in Goethe's life and work comes much to the same conclusion as R. Friedenthal. Karl Viëtor, on the contrary, echoes Goethe's own intention when he says that the author's aim was to show "the basic truth of his existence," i.e., the inner rather than the outer truth.

This becomes strikingly apparent when we compare the number of pages of the various parts. Parts one and three consist of 232 pages each, part two of 249 pages, part four of a mere 121 pages. The individual *books* in part one through three fluctuate between 33 and 57 pages (only two *books* have less than 40 pages) while in part four the individual *books* contain 17, 19, 25, 28, and 29 pages. Each part terminates in an apocalyptic experience.

The thematic structure–though following the usual chronological order (birth, infancy, childhood, adolescence, adulthood)–is organized with extreme care. Goethe uses for its development his concept of organic growth. This concept, the result of intense studies of natural history, forms a rather substantial part of all of Goethe's work and thought. The account of his life opens in the grand dramatic style of classical tragedy. Twelve noon, the sun in the sign of the Virgin was at its highest point–Jupiter and Venus smiling at him, Mercury looking on not adversely, while Saturn and Mars remained indifferent. The moon was just waxing full so that the birth could not take place till its hour was up (*D&W*, pt. 1, p. 15).[16]

The richness of the symbolism in this first paragraph is overwhelming. Goethe, like Wordsworth standing at the cross-roads, convinced of his own greatness, stages his entrance into this world accordingly. It is not a new dawn, he is being born into, but high noon. The time was ripe. Hundreds of writers had prepared his way for centuries, painfully slow, step by step. Goethe was to put the crown on all their previous achievements. The time was ripe. Jupiter and Venus were smiling. Jupiter reigning high above the struggling and squirming multitudes, smiling at the birth of his favorite son. Surely, this is a projection of the later Goethe frowning or smiling benignly from his Olympian Heights in Weimar at the countless disciples whose pilgrimage led them to his house. It is well known that Venus had been smiling on him all his life whether in the guise of Kätchen (Schönkopf), Friedericke (Brion), Lotte (Buff), Maxe (Brentano), Lili (Schönemann), Charlotte (von Stein), Christiane (Vulpius), Minna (Herzlieb), Marianne (von Willemer), Ulricke (von Levetzow), and

16 Heinrich Meyer points out that when Goethe writes fiction (erfindet) then he needs great opera scenes, theater scenery, greater then life imagery. *Die Kunst des Erzählens*, Bern, Francke Verlags-AG., 1972, p. 76.

quite a few other members of the fairer sex who had crossed his path. It was Venus' smile that inspired the young, the middle-aged, and even the octagenarian[17] to write his greatest works, his finest lyrics. Mercury was also always there to do his bidding. Only Mars and Saturn, the masters of war and violence, remained indifferent, the two elements utterly alien to Goethe's thought and work. The stage was well prepared for the triumphal arrival of the gods' favorite son. But while the gods smiled, human inadequacy almost spoiled the great moment and all the elaborate preparations. The midwife, inadequately trained for emergencies, delivered a still-born baby. Only intense and continued efforts brought life into the infant. Goethe, making the most of this detail, dramatically attributes his preservation to the favorable constellation of the stars and planets.[18] But while the stars had favored the revival efforts on their favorite son, his paternal grandfather, magistrate of Frankfurt, took more immediate action and initiated a midwife training program, which was to prevent similar calamities for future babies. Subtly and shrewdly the aged Goethe, fully convinced of his patriarchal role, extended in *Dichtung und Wahrheit* the beneficial influence he sought to exert upon mankind to the very first moment of his life.

Family members and home supply the initial impressions and experiences for the baby. Goethe is most careful in formulating these, but as he points out:

> If one tries to remember what occurred during our earliest youth, it happens quite frequently that one is apt to confuse that which we have heard from others with what we possess from our own personal experience. (*D&W.*, p. 15).

(Rousseau and Wordsworth had experienced much the same dilemma, though the latter acknowledged it, while the former abandoned himself to emotional and nostalgic reveries.) Growing older, young

---

17 It was Ulricke who inspired him to write *Marienbader Elegien* in the years 1829-31, poems full of youthful ardor and emotions.

18 What a contrast to Rousseau's description of his birth: "I was born handicapped and sick; I cost my mother her life, and my birth was the first of my misfortunes" (Rousseau, *op. cit.*, p. 7). One man is intent to underline the beginning of a life of fulfillment and content, and the other of hardship and miseries.

Goethe leaves the home and explores the town. Frankfurt reveals itself to the adventurous youth in all its splendour, and the writer recreates some forty-five to fifty years later the emotional impact that each discovery, each adventure had on the youthful mind. Friends, fantasy and daydreams, youthful pranks contribute to his growth; schooling and his father's systematic tutoring and prodding further and complement that growth. Farther and farther the young man ventures away from home: excursions to surrounding suburbs and then, at the tender age of sixteen, student life at Leipzig where a well-renowned faculty was expected to complete his formal education and further his intellectual development.

Goethe's education there or any place else was anything but bookish. After three years and a considerable metamorphosis, illness forces him to return to Frankfurt. The element of physical suffering is added to his multiple experiences. A short but very profitable stay in Strassburg follows his recuperation, during which he earns his Licentiate in Jurisprudence, makes Herder's acquaintance and, under his expert guidance, learns to appreciate the beauty of gothic architecture. A journey to Switzerland follows his engagement to Lili and intense mental torment, and finally his permanent departure from Frankfurt completes the four books of *Dichtung und Wahrheit*. This, in essence, is Goethe's life as we find it in his work.

Goethe's was not an aimless and grueling odyssey, in which the traveler is being thrown by fate from trial to ecstacy to trial, but according to *Dichtung und Wahrheit*, it was a well outlined and scrupulously followed path. Surely it offered a fair amount of snares and stones, of delightful surprises and unexpected crevasses.

> "For all the birds there is a bait and every human being is led and misled in his own way." (*D&W*, pt. 1, p. 182).

But at the end of this path the reader finds the man, Goethe, the accomplished individual evolved from this nearly dead—born infant which, nevertheless, had contained a complete assortment of human potentials, ready and waiting to be developed, each at its proper moment, all in their proper sequence. Contrary to Rousseau who perceives himself to be thrown helplessly and without recourse hither and thither by a blind fate, Goethe believes in a firm necessity which

138

governs human development and life.

Goethe's parting from Frankfurt in part four, marks a permanent farewell to home and family in 1775 and the beginning of his dual professional career at the Ducal Court at Weimar. Repeatedly the poet expressed his intention to continue the work which encompasses only the first twenty-five years of his life, but, though he subtitles "The Italian Voyage," "The Siege of Mainz," and the "Campagne in France" *From My Life*, these writings represent only isolated experiences which lack the continuity and the unity of an autobiography.

We have already seen that Goethe's conception of his work went considerably beyond the established limitations of the conventional autobiography. After having completed part three, the author indicated that *Dichtung und Wahrheit* is by no means the "spontaneous overflow" of fond memories or powerful recollections, but that it represents a work carfully structured according to the laws underlying the "metamorphoses of the plants."[19] Part one was to show the child developing its tender roots into all directions with very little leaves; in the second part the boy is seen with more lively greening and branching out on different levels, while part three must bring him to the blooming stage, showing the promising young man. Although in the end Goethe did not quite adhere to this plan, this underlying organic design is quite obvious, the branching out, the absorbing of nourishment from earth and air, and the resulting accompanying multi-dimensional growth. Despite its exposure to hail and snow, storm and rain, but also to its share of sun and warmth, the plant, rooted in favorable soil and tended with a fair share of care, will profit from each of these conditions. The cold will make it hardy, its roots must reach deep and grow strong if it is not to be destroyed and blown over by the first November storm. The weak seedling will wither and succumb to the storms.

Here the philosopher is at work, much more so than the autobiographer. The pedagogue with a message and a mission shows "that which is generally valid" and applicable. "Goethe has nothing to confess," Friedenthal tells us, "he does not surprise us with "truths." He does not try to surprise us at all, either by the exposure of vices and

---

19 Goethe, *Werke*, Cotta Jubiläumsausgabe, Vol. XXIV, p. 267. Cf. also Viétor, *op. cit.*, p. 220.

moral transgressions, or by psychological flashes throwing a "new light" on hitherto unsuspected facets of his "inner life."[20] But he does show the need and the importance of a sound and close family life, of guidance, discipline and order, of tradition and historical perspective if the infant is to grow into a happy, well-rounded human being.

In his autobiographical work Goethe has poetically developed and transformed a number of incidents and experiences from his youth in order to give them apocalyptic or catapulting importance. Each incident marks the closing of an important phase in his life and prepares him, after a time of more or less extreme suffering and dejection, for his next phase of development, the opening of new vistas. Each time a new dimension is added to the man. Although some of these events do not appear to have the apocalyptic character at the moment they happen, future developments as presented in the work substantiate in every instance that they had been just that. In some instances it takes an extended period of time before the existing problems or dilemmas can be completely resolved.

Again representative examples have been chosen in order to show how Goethe, like his French and British counterparts, skillfully combining autobiographical detail with imaginative poetic creation, transformed initially minor events into elaborate and far-reaching experiences of major structural importance in the thematic development of his work.

Little do we know about the immediate or the actual long-range influence Grandmother Goethe had upon Johann and his younger sister. Yet in the work both her life and—in a quite different way— her death are shown to have had far-reaching consequences in the development of the child. We learn that the children usually spent their leisure hours in her spacious living room, where Grandmother always knew how to entertain them.

> One Christmas Evening, however, she crowned all her good deeds by presenting us with a puppet show, and so created a new world in the old house. The unexpected spectacle exerted powerful attraction upon our young minds. It made an especially profound impression upon the boy, an im-

20 Richard Friedenthal, *Goethe: His Life and Times,* Cleveland, The World Publishing Company, 1963, p. 419.

pression which long afterwards continued its great reverberations. (*D&W*, pt. 1, p. 20).

It was grandmother's last legacy, for shortly after the holidays she died. It cannot be said that either her death or the gift of the puppet theater were, properly speaking, of an apocalyptic or catapulting nature, although both brought about great changes in the boy's development and daily life. Yet, considering the long-range effects as developed and presented in the autobiographical work, they must be considered as such. The gift introduces young Goethe to the magic of the theater, first as a delighted spectator and later, when the stage with its actors is turned over to the children, it becomes the source of endless hours of entertainment, a challenge to the children's own fantasy and talents. It laid the very foundation for Goethe's infatuation with the theater, both as a playwright and an actor. It most certainly led young Goethe to become an avid and regular visitor of Frankfurt's theaters well before he had reached the age of ten.

Important as the puppet show may have been in developing Goethe's interest in and love for the theater, the grandmother's death seems—at least as far as the elaborate structure of the work is concerned—to have had even greater and far-reaching consequences. Up to this time, young Goethe and his sister Cornelia had been largely confined to the house and garden (*D&W*, pt. 1). Their social intercourse was limited to family and servants, carefully selected tutors, and a few friends of the family. It was a closed, confined circle. The children were closely supervised and their activities carefully regulated. Grandmother's death, however, was to change all this. First, it set in motion elaborate remodeling plans for the two adjacent homes, plans which father Goethe had carefully drawn up over a number of years. He had not been able to put them into practice because of his mother's adamant refusal of change. Now, after her death, walls were torn down, doors and windows changed, and the roof was literally lifted off the two houses, opening new vistas and adding new dimensions. Father Goethe had decided to stay in the house in order to better supervise the job himself. This, of course, meant considerable inconvenience and a thorough disruption of the otherwise well regulated and smooth running household. Both, supervision and discipline, normally paramount in the daily routine of the Goethe children, were slackened. The children, maybe for the first time in their lives, were often on their own and it was at this time that young Wolfgang, taking full advantage of the situation, becomes for the first time aware of his hometown. In a series of fantastically colorful, vibrant genre paintings, the poet recreates in his work his old, proud hometown, rich in old customs and traditions, with its activities, durable nay indestructable, which celebrates an imperial coronation and endures a French occupation with equal magnanimity. The boy discovers (and in turn the reader) that the Frankfurt of his days represents the culmination of 2000 years of rich cultural and intellectual development. It is a miniature republic where moral law and order, social and intellectual consciousness flourish, where excess of any kind is suspect and frowned upon, where men live, active and prospering, a dignified, harmonious and tranquil existence. The marketplace, the various festivities the author evokes before our eyes are worthy of the brush of a Ghirlandaio, an Altdorfer.

Much emphasis in part one is placed on the development of sensory perception, while part two stresses primarily the adolescent's intellectual growth. Consciously or subconsciously the young man is continually driven toward new sights, new sounds, the not-yet-experienced. Insatiably he aborbs every new view, every new sound or smell his hometown has to offer. Emotionally and intellectually we see him often aloof and reluctant to commit himself to anything definite up to the very last part of the book. He is not ready for output. His life at the age of fifteen--in fact up to his final departure from Frankfurt--is all intake. Observations and expositions, strewn in here and there, are--and Goethe is most careful to point this out--given from the narrator's point of view after 1811. "My age," the narrator tells us while describing the coronation festivites, "prevented me from meditating extensively" (D&W, pt. 1, p. 228). Contemplation and meditation will be reserved for the older Goethe. The fifteen-year-old, in the meantime, is daily fascinated and enthralled by new discoveries, new experiences, to which Grandmother Goethe's death had first opened the doors.

We know from Goethe's letters, diary entries, etc., that these colorful scenes owed their inclusion in the work not to an exceptional facility for remembering past impressions and experiences, but to the diligent research of the creatively active poet. In retrospect, he is recreating an era and a place which he feels decisively influenced his future development. Though he may not be able to recall individual details some fifty years later, the substratum to his present personality was laid by similar, though maybe not identical, remote impressions and experiences during his early youth. The discussion of one such description may serve as an example for countless similar ones throughout the work, where the creating artist and not the autobiographer prevails.

A number of traditional festivities, some of them dating back centuries, punctuated the course of each year in Frankfurt. The *Pfeifergericht* is one of these. A large number of cities annually sends special envoys to pay homage and tribute to the Magistrate of Frankfurt during a special ceremony. Since the boy's grandfather was Magistrate at the time, the event–bestowing a certain aura of distinction on his ancestry–was, quite understandably, of special significance to Goethe. Consequently he develops it–just like De Quincey had done with his dream-visions–with meticulous care. Some previously developed themes and outlined impressions converge during the decisive moment of the account, highlighting, reinforcing, and dramatizing it (*D&W*, pt. 1, Bk. i). On a previous occasion, the reader had accompanied young Goethe to the *Römer*, famed City Hall, where Emperors and Electors enjoyed their meals following the Imperial Elections. The great Emperor's Hall with its portraits of all the Emperors of the Holy Roman Empire had particularly fascinated the boy. The *Pfeifergericht*-ceremony is taking place in this very same hall. The town dignitaries are already seated, each according to his social rank. The *Schöffengericht* (court of lay assessors) is in session. The sentences are being read. Goethe, the playwright, has set the stage again. The great scene is about to begin:

> Suddenly strange music announces, so-to-speak, the arrival of bygone centuries. Three musicians enter with wind instruments, one with an old shawm, the second with a bass, and the third one with a *pommer* or oboe. They are wearing blue coats, trimmed in gold, the music fastened to their sleeves, and their heads covered. This is how, at ten o'clock sharp, they had stepped out of their inn, envoys and attendants behind them, marvelled at by natives and strangers alike. And this is how they enter the Hall. The court procedures are stopped. Musicians and attendants remain

before the barrier, the envoy enters and comes face to face with the Mayor. The symbolic offerings, exacted precisely in accordance with old tradition, consisted generally of such items as the offering town was wont to trade in. Pepper was symbolic of all goods, and the envoy brought on this occasion a beautifully wrought cup filled with pepper. Over it were spread a pair of gloves, strangely slit, trimmed and tasselled in silk, as a sign of a granted and acknowledged privilege which even the Emperor used on certain occasions. Next to it one could see a small rod which was formerly never missing during official or judicial events. A few small silver coins were also included, and the city of Worms brought an old felt hat, redeeming it again and again, so that for many years it was a witness to these ceremonies. (*D&W*, pt. 1, p. 31).

The entire scene, though thoroughly anchored in contemporary everyday business (the court in session), transposes the reader momentarily back to the Middle Ages, a time of elaborate pageants, ceremonious encounters, and colorful costumes. Deliberately the poet recreates at length a very picturesque folkloric scene which even in the days of his youth was in striking contrast with contemporary life. The spectators—not only the very conservative and sober "natives," but even the strangers who, during their travels, must have encountered many strange and marvelous sights--they all stopped and "bestaunten," i.e., gaped or wondered at this strange procession. Though the *Pfeifergericht* is of longstanding tradition, kept alive by the city, the fuller meaning of the ceremony evades many bystanders so that it really has lost much of its initially concrete impact. And the author deliberately creates the impression of a fairytale episode. The suddenness of the "strange music" produced on archaic instruments, the musicians' unusual attire, the fact that they could stand in the presence of such important company without removing their hats, all these elements convey an impression of a fleeting illusion, a vision. The fact that not one word alludes to a single purely human attribute of any one individual in this procession, intensifies this impression. They could be marionettes going through a series of symbolic gestures which to them have lost purpose and meaning, while the blood and flesh participants have—for the duration of this spectacle—been frozen in their actions. The poet, creating this fleeting miniature vision (and countless similar ones), enables the reader to glimpse back through the centuries at history. In many respects these visions

144

bear a certain similarity to those experienced by De Quincey under the influence of opium. The important difference, as far as the autobiographical genre is concerned, lies not in their thematic difference, but in the fact that Goethe's poetic genius enabled him to create such visions, while De Quincey's--with the help of opium--imposed themselves on his consciousness. The fact that Goethe was trying to give this episode a certain ephemeral, ghost-like quality, can best be felt in the one-sentence paragraph which concludes this ceremony:

> After the envoy had made his speech, delivered his present, and had received from the Mayor the assurance of continuing patronage, he withdrew from the closed circle, the musicians played, the procession left as it had come in, the court pursued its business, until the second and finally the third envoy were led in . . . . (D&W, pt. 1, p. 31).

Seven active verbs in rapid succession, often with a blatantly bare direct object (speech, present, assurance), twice even without that (played, left) are designed to speed up the action, to bring the scene to an abrupt close. The spook is gone. The Schöffengericht resumes its activities as if nothing had happened. The magic "circle" is closed again impervious to this and similar interruptions. The incident the poet evoked was vivid and colorful, but--like millions of similar incidents in a human life--fleeting and subject to fall into oblivion. But the aged Goethe believes firmly that somehow, somewhere such incidents had left their indelible imprints on his life and personality.

There are numerous instances where we see the expert writer manipulate his subject matter for the sake of variety or suspense. When during the Seven-Year-War a French Detachment, sent to assist the Imperial Troops, was assigned quarters in the pro-Prussian Goethe household, a confrontation between the head of the household, Rat Goethe, and the head of the detachment, Königslieutenant Count de Thoranc, seemed inevitable. Young Goethe was not present when his father found the long-awaited opportune moment to insult the officer. Nor was he present, when the interpreter, a long-standing friend of the Goethe family, pleaded with the Count to spare the family. Yet Goethe, braking with autobiographical tradition, makes these pages of Dichtung und Wahrheit sparkle with lively and spontaneous dialogue confronting justified but uncontrolled anger with the calm dictates of reason and humaneness. The reader, because of the vividness of the dialogue, feels himself transposed into the chambers and the very presence of De Thoranc. With this very simple method the author accomplishes three things: 1. He very effectively completes the character portrait of Count de Thoranc which he had already carefully developed in the preceding pages. The poet had shown him as a wise, intelligent human being, not devoid of warmth, charity, and compassion. This act of forgiveness underlines all these qualities. Hearing the words of the Count himself leaves the reader with a more vivid, more immediate impression, than a mere description of the person would have conveyed; 2. The writer, sensing the somewhat slow pace of the narrative at this point (which could lead to the loss of the reader's interest), injects life and new momentum into his story; 3. the poet effectively heightens and sustains suspense uninterruptedly throughout the three and one half page episode (*D&W*, Bk. 3, pp. 114-118) during which Rat Goethe's life hangs in the balance, until the Count, appeased by the interpreter's arguments, declares somewhat impatiently yet with magnanimity: "We have wasted too many words already; go now–let the ingrate thank you–I shall spare him!" This, indeed, is ultimate greatness of mind. Not "he can come to thank me!" No, "let him thank you" (*D&W*, Bk. 3, p. 118).

Marginally the narrator wonders whether these were the exact words of wisdom the interpreter used, or whether the man embellished the scene "as one is wont to do after a fortunate and good experience."[21] The reader, however, may wonder whether anybody, even a Goethe, has the memory to recall such a lengthy dialogue– even after having heard it dozens of times–after an interval of fifty-some years. The event was rather unimportant in view of the author's life and development. Yet the narrator developed it to an event of central importance in book three of his work. Besides the purpose of structural development, it gave the poet an opportunity to fully develop a character portrait of, what he considered, a truly noble human being–*die schöne Seele*– who acts graciously and justly under the most trying circumstances, regardless whether with friend or foe.

If Grandmother's death had in a very symbolic manner opened the doors onto the world, another event of apocalyptic nature

21 *Dichtung und Wahrheit*, Bk. 3, p. 118.

brought about a very dramatic confrontation between God—Christianity—and the experimenting youngster.

At the time of the Lisbon earthquake in 1755 young Goethe was merely six years old. Yet again the event had a very deep and far-reaching effect on the child:

> Through an extraordinary universal event the peace of mind of the boy was for the first time deeply troubled. (*D&W*, Bk. 1, p. 36).

Listening to the horror tales of the catastrophe which had befallen the just and unjust, the wicked and the innocent, the youngster tried in vain to reconcile such an event with his notion of a wise and benevolent God, the Creator and Preserver of heaven and earth. A rather minor event, certainly in no way comparable to the Lisbon disaster, but because of its immediacy and personal involvement of even greater importance to the boy, was a severe hailstorm in the following summer. This hailstorm destroyed a number of large glass windows in the just remodeled Goethe residence and did considerable damage to furniture and books. The servants went into an extreme state of panic. Crying and praying, the crouched in the dark hallway and pulled the young boy down with them on his knees, hoping to appease in such manner "the angered deity." Again the boy felt the wrath of an angry God, punishing without discrimination. Of even greater surprise must have been the relationship (in this case of utter wrath and abject terror) which he observed during these terrifying moments between God the Father and His Children. Obviously the six-year-old did not resolve the religious question at this point. But the aging Goethe brings these incidents vividly alive some fifty-odd years later, showing the reader that they constituted for him the beginning of a rather extended period of intense preoccupation with Christian religious teachings and an effort to reach his own personal relationship and understanding with God and Christianity. The various stages of the search comprised conventional religious instruction, the aforementioned personal experiences and the ritual building of an altar in honor of the Creator of all nature in the manner of the Old Testament. "Products of nature were to represent the world in proxy and a flame, representing man's aspiring heart toward its creator, was to rise from it" (*D&W*, pt. 1, p. 50). Unfortunately young Goethe had used a precious lacquered table to offer his sacrifice, and the heat damaged the delicate finish. The older Goethe, recreating this very colorful and touching scene, uses the dire outcome of this first sacrificial ceremony as an excuse, to comment and warn against such means of approach toward God.

Goethe had arrived at an emotionally satisfying concept of religion for himself by the end of part one. In part two he settles the question intellectually.

> I built myself a Christianity for my own private use, trying to construct it with the exact study of history and to substantiate it by exact observation of those who had shown a penchant for my ideas. (*D&W*, p. 695).

In part four we find him again extensively preoccupied with the religious question, in particular with questions of faith. But it is no longer a personal, emotional search, but rather a rational-historical approach to the major characters and their actions in the Old Testament.

> No matter how humane, beautiful and serene the religion of the Patriarchs appears, it is laced with traits of savageness and cruelty, out of which man may emerge or into which he may return. (*D&W*, p. 151).

Personal search had led to metaphysical speculations which in turn gave way to a historical examination of the development of mankind so intricately connected with a variety of religions.[22] This can be observed in a number of reflections and musings such as the following: The Gods "in order to tempt us, seem to bring to the fore these characteristics that man is inclined to attribute to them," and they order man (in this case Abraham) to commit monstrous acts. A rather paradoxical statement, linking with one vast sweep remote past and present moment, the biblical Patriarch with eighteenth-century mankind, which though separated by a long and often tumultuous history, remain nevertheless identical by virtue of their human essence.

That the basic religious issues had been satisfactorily resolved on the emotional as well as on the intellectual level at a relatively early

22 Heinrich Meyer refers to *Dichtung und Wahrheit* as the work in which Goethe established a parallel between his own life and the development of mankind in a context of religious history (Goethe, *das Leben im Werk, op. cit.*, p. 459).

stage can best be seen from numerous indications throughout the work. But Goethe remained preoccupied with religious questions throughout his life. He studied, in fact, a number of religions. Several attempts were made at different times by well-meaning friends and representatives of different sects to convert him to their way of thinking. Again and again he turned to great works whose authors had chosen biblical events as their basic theme. But God, religion, or faith constitutes no longer subjective involvement, or a *"crise de con-science,"* but merely historical interest:

> In the contentment of youth, I was inclined toward a sort of optimism. I had reconciled myself with God and the gods, for in the course of the years I had reached the conclusion that there was many a counterbalance against evil, that one could be restored from depravity, and that one could extract oneself from danger and without necessarily having to break one's neck. (*D&W*, p. 179).

Goethe's religious attitude and relationship to God were best summed up in Part II, Book four, at a time when nature assumed ever greater importance in his daily life:

> Surely there is no more beautiful adoration of the Deity than that for which we need no image, but which arises in our bosom exclusively from our dialogue with nature. (*D&W*, p. 247).[23]

Again, we can watch here the poet/philosopher at work. He uses a universally known event of disastrous proportions and consequences as a catapult which launches and explains his interest in and preoccupation with religion. Surely, every reader has experienced similar doubts when a natural—or in these last decades a man-made--catastrophe annihilates entire villages or towns. Usually, however, such thoughts evoked by distant events are effaced by matters of more immediate concern. Only a very personal experience with disastrous consequences would keep such thoughts alive and would probably lead to deeper probing. Goethe supplies such an incident with the vivid description of a thundering hailstorm. Again the reader can identify with the feelings of utter terror displayed by the servants'

---

23 Here and in many similar passages Goethe acknowledges that the Romantic movement had left its indelible marks on his thoughts, although he adamantly refused to be identified with it.

action and behavior. Such cosmic events like the earth-quake and the hailstorm, because of their unpredictability, remind man most forcibly of his limitations and helplessness. In such moments of terror and distress his thoughts turn to God, the Father, in hopes of protection and salvation.

Though there must have been talk about the Lisbon disaster in the Goethe household, it is very unlikely that such discussions would have led the youngster to ponder such questions as God's justice and God's love. It is also highly questionable whether the servant's abject terror during the thunderstorm led the six-year-old to doubt the conventionally taught and accepted doctrines of Christianity. We notice that the terror was not apparent on the members of the Goethe family, i.e., his father, mother, and sister. The servants, presumably because their lack of intellectual understanding, responded in a very elemental, emotional way, submitting to–what to them must have seemed–a punishment for some dark, obscure sin. Yet the boy at this tender age certainly would react in the same elemental way, terrified and helpless, as he watched the new window panes being shattered by the hail stones.

Both incidents, however, by virtue of their universal symbolism, make ideal starting points for the writer who is developing this theme --in this instance his preoccupations with religion--in a logically structured, escalating form. To accept either incident as an autobiographical apocalyptic experience, would be unrealistic.

The third important event–the first one to show immediate consequences--coincides with the coronation of Emperor Joseph II (*D&W*, Bk. 5, pp. 197-237). The choice of time and place was again of symbolic importance for the overall structure of the work. An imperial coronation in 1764 with all its accompanying elaborate preparations, the colourful visitors from near and far, and finally the stream of endless festivities, represented for many of the people from Frankfurt the culminating and most unforgettable experience of their life. The lowliest of the citizenry could glimpse for one short moment the splendor and pageantry surrounding the life of the emperor and his entourage, while the upper classes of the town partook in it themselves. Carnival mood prevailed among the multicolored masses that had streamed into town for the occasion. Young

150

Goethe's emotions and passions had also reached a high pitch. He is almost sixteen years old. Exhilarated by his first love and animated by the friendship he was cultivating secretly, he joined the festivities with his friends.

> We spent the greatest part of the night in a most enjoyable and happy way in a feeling of friendship, love, and inclination. When I accompanied Gretchen to her door she kissed me on the forehead. It was the first and the last time that she bestowed on me such a favor: unfortunately I was never to see her again. (*D&W*, Bk. 5, p. 230)

Though the language of the sexagenarian Goethe does not exactly do justice to the initial impact that such a kiss has on a passionate fifteen-year-old, the creating artist's elaborate background development and the ensuing consequences bring it out quite clearly. In the work, the conclusion of the elaborate and highly emotional festivities coincides with the abrupt end of both his friendship and his love and plunges young Goethe in the deepest depression of his young life.

Gretchen had been Goethe's first great love. His heart had been aflame from almost the very first moment of their encounter. Again he erected an altar—as he was wont to do during his long life on numerous occasions—and kept the candles burning day and night. Again considerable damage resulted, not to a brightly lacquered table, but this time to his young and vulnerable heart. Although Gretchen, "incredibly beautiful," the object of his dreams for several months, did not seem to have shared his passion, she represents the first of a series of females who played a formative role in Goethe's life. As exemplified in his play *Iphigenie*, the poet venerated The Woman in a way reminiscent of the old Germanic tribes. It is she who heals the wounds that life inflicts upon the male, she tempers his rash impulses, quiets his tempestuousness, softens his crudeness. She is the means by which man will be enabled to attain a truly humane state.[24] In *Dichtung und Wahrheit* it is Gretchen who

---

24 Once Goethe got carried away and tried to embrace her. She told him then: "Don't kiss me! there is something vulgar about it; but cherish me, if it is possible." When questioned by the police about their relationship, she stated, much to the consternation of the young man, that she looked upon him as a child and loved him like a brother.

dissuades young Goethe from writing prank love letters to a young maiden, when her cousins and their friends had decided to put his poetic talents to "good" use. Fully aware that for the youngsters it is nothing more than a harmless joke, she nevertheless commiserates with the poor young girl they were about to dupe. In retrospect--and many years later--the poet appreciates her efforts. As he is wont to do, he sees the beneficial consequences not only of this particular experience, but of all ensuing experiences of a similar nature:

> Nature seems to determine that one sex becomes sensuously aware of the good and the beautiful in the other sex. And so it was that the sight of her and my inclination for her opened for me a new world of beauty and excellence. (D&W, pt. 2, p. 189).

Apparently the young people he befriended came from the very lowest social strata of the rigidly structured Frankfurt society, and Goethe had been most anxious to keep his intercourse with them secret. Since all of them were obliged to work in order to earn a living (Gretchen, he discovered to his dismay, worked as a milliner's helper), their encounters were limited to late evening gatherings when Goethe either joined them at their modest home or they went to a small inn, obscure enough not to risk any chance encounters with his friends and family.

Though acutely aware that his friends would never be socially acceptable to his family, young Goethe worries little about class distinction at the time of the coronation. He feels utterly secure in his love and their friendship as they spend the evening of the coronation festivities together, watching and participating, admiring the splendor of the various elaborate displays put on by the local and visiting nobility and courts. "By fours we went most contentedly to and fro," he writes in *Dichtung und Wahrheit* "myself at Gretchen's side, and I imagined myself to be wandering through the happy Elysian Fields" (D&W, pt. 2, p. 230). To culminate the events of the day and to epitomize his happiness, Gretchen--and he always uses the endearing diminutive form for Margarete--had kissed him on the forehead.

The next morning, however, brought a terrible and sobering awakening. Apparently the friends had misused his trust. One of the young men, who--at young Goethe's urging--had been given a position in the town hall, was in jail for embezzlement and fraud. Confined to his room till the extent of his involvement was determined, the young adolescent abandons himself in passionate loneliness to his intense sorrow and self-accusations. Betrayed, deserted, and misunderstood, he withdraws from the world and society. The emotional shock of the events, the intense turmoil that followed them, proves too overwhelming and young Goethe becomes violently ill. Part one of the work concludes very effectively with Gretchen's departure from Frankfurt, Goethe's terrible emotional state, and his poor physical condition.

During this first part we have watched the boy grow up to adolescence and to unfold the complete range of his emotions and sensations from bare awareness to the highest as well as the lowest pitch on the emotional scale. His religious impressions were as much on the emotional level as were his theatrical ones. The rich pictorial scenes from the town, excursions, and lastly the coronation pageant were as sensuous in their appeal as the contemptuously drawn details of the mob scenes when wine and food, and finally gold and silver coins were distributed during the festivities. It is the consciously creating artist who conjures the scenery of such tremendously emotional impact against which the passions (both joy and suffering) of the individual are being mirrored. The sexagenarian may have lost the facility to relive and to recreate the emotional intensity of the adolescent's passions, but the artist has not lost his ability to create the proper historical setting where they can develop and flourish. The historical considerations and the moral implications inherent in such events are offered by the sixty-two year old poet and were not experienced by the adolescent. They were the work of the old Goethe, the polished writer and seasoned philosopher. Contrary to Wordsworth who made the historical event (the Revolution) the turning point in his life, Goethe uses it (the Coronation) as a very effective background for a very passionate, personal, and individual drama. The boy from a first timid and curious peeking out from behind the curtain of life, has become part of it. He had known the security of a sheltered life and the fear in the face of an angered God. He had learned to be happy, to be sad, to trust and to distrust, to admire and to loathe, to accept and to condemn, above all he had learned to love in a most innocent, but in a most violent way and now he had to suffer, to suffer as intensely, as abysmally and hopelessley as only a sixteen-year-old can suffer.[25] But he would recover. He would love again, though never as ecstatically as the first time, he would find other friends, yet never again would he bestow upon them this same extensive and unlimited trust for he would always remember his suffering. By the same token, he would never again suffer quite as intensely, for there was now the knowledge that even the most intense suffering would eventually come to an end.

If the first part of the work had been structured to show the development of the child's animal instincts, an awareness as well as the gradual evolution of his emotions and social and historical consciousness, the second part (pp. 241-388) traces Goethe's rational and aesthetic formation.

Richard Friedenthal makes a rather strong case in his Goethe biography for his notion that the experience of Goethe's Leipzig sojourn did by far fall short of the implied results in *Dichtung und Wahrheit*. What Friedenthal does--like so many before him--is to compare notes (Goethe's own letters of the period, eyewitness accounts of fellow students, teachers, and acquaintances) in order to show discrepancies in Goethe's autobiography. The problem here, of course, is that Mr. Friedenthal overlooks the fact that we are dealing here with a literary work rather than with a conventional, largely factual autobiography.

Just as we have watched a young Goethe develop his sensual perception, his emotional spiritual growth in part one, we follow his intellectual/rational and aesthetic development in the second part. Finding himself now in search of new dimensions, however, did not mean the elimination of previous acquirements; rather he was adding to the already existing ones. Graphically we could probably best visualize the development in the various parts like this:

25 "First love is rightly said to be the only one: for in the second and through the second the lofty sense of love is already lost. The notion of the eternal and the infinite, which initially elevates and carries it, is destroyed. It seems transitory like all recurrent things" *Dichtung und Wahrheit*, p. 632.

essence and   childhood   pubescence   adolescence
potentialities

The small dot represents both essence and potentialities. Each additional concentric circle is one area of experience, one developed potential, enriching, increasing forever the original dot as the individual strives to add yet another circle, another dimension. In the end it is, therefore, of small consequence whether the author renames his Leipzig Käthchen Ännchen in the work, whether his appreciation of Winckelmann's writings commenced at such and such a particular time in Leipzig or not, whether he adhered during his student days there to his now classical formula of "noble simplicity and quiet grandeur" (edle Einfalt stille Grösse) or, on the contrary, dressed like a young fop, imitating the fashion dictates of the day. These things are really immaterial to the spirit of the work. But we must at all times remember that it is "poetry and truth." Karl Viëtor comes much closer to an understanding in his appraisal of the work:

> A great human being attempts to show the deployment of the I as an exemplary case of human growth. An individual with a strong sense of independence wants to develop the inherent potentials with which he has been equipped in constant intercourse with his surroundings.[26]

In part two the added dimension to this already established intercourse is of an intellectual and aesthetic nature. This does not

26 Karl Viëtor, *op. cit.*, pp. 219-220.

mean that the young man will no longer participate in student pranks and railleries, or shun the company of the fairer sex. This, in fact, is one of the pleasures that Goethe refused to forego during his entire life. The octagenarian was still as intensely delighted in the company of a fair maiden, as the teenager had been during his student days. But the young man in *Dichtung und Wahrheit* had come to Leipzig to pursue primarily--though not exclusively--the intellectual and aesthetic aspects of his education.

The university of Leipzig enjoyed considerable renown around 1765. It had been Rat Goethe's decision that his son should study law there. As it so frequently happens, the son felt quite strongly about choosing a course of studies and of life which coincided with his own interests rather than with his father's wishes. And for this Leipzig offered ample opportunity.

"Gallant Leipzig," the town itself, renowned for its international fairs, modern, spacious and elegant, resplendant in its Baroque architecture, provided a striking contrast to the walled-in medieval Frankfurt with its narrow streets and dark alleys. The university had among its faculty some of the greatest German minds of the time: Hofrat Böhme, Gellert, Gessler, and Wieland, to name only a few.[27] Besides pursuing studies in English, French, and Classical literature, Goethe made at that time the acquaintance of such modern German authors as Bodmer, Haller, Ramler, Lessing, and Wieland. Literature became an increasingly more important aspect of his life. As time passed, he devoted less and less time to the study of law and more and more time to the fine arts. As a consequence, he digresses in this part of the work frequently into the realm of literature:

> If I have put my readers with these cursatory and desultory remarks about German literature into a state of confusion, I succeeded in giving a picture of the chaotic condition in which my poor mind found itself, when, in the conflict of two for the literary fatherland tremendously important periods, so many new things pressed upon me, before I had the time to come to terms with the old ones; at a time, when so much of the old exerted its

27 Again, the student Goethe probably paid as little attention to them at the time as Wordsworth to his studies in Cambridge. But the mature Goethe, having realized the importance of these men's contribution to literature, reserved them a place in his autobiographical work.

right upon me, when I already had thought to have reason enough to discard it completely. (*D&W*, pt. 2, p. 310)

But his interests were by no means limited to literature. The artist Adam Friedrich Oeser (1717-1799), both friend and teacher, aroused his curiosity for the classical concepts of art by introducing him to Winckelmann's writings which reached Leipzig from Rome, where the latter was curator of the Vatican art treasures. The eager young Goethe was also introduced to the art of etching and he studied diligently the secrets and finer points of this art. His interests at that time were multifaceted and of the most diverse nature. After visiting the art galleries in Dresden, we see him dabbling in drawing and etching. Also, he was pampered by a number of elderly matrons, and, as behooves a young man of his age, we see him involved in a fleeting romance or two. He is stimulated and assaulted by an ever changing flux of impressions, thoughts, and preoccupations. Theological discussions are followed by philosophical ones. Lovers' quarrels follow amor's conquests. He wrote occasional verses and two plays which survived his mania for the periodical burning of his juvenile work.[28] On the whole, precious little thought and time had been given to what initially was to be his main purpose for coming to Leipzig: the study of law.

> The university where I missed the objective of my family and even my own, was to give me a foundation of that in which I was fo find the greatest contentment of my life. (*D&W*, pt. 2, p. 348).

Goethe realized his shortcomings, but he was far from regretting them. Had it not been for another apocalyptic event, he might have continued this rather agreeable, stimulating, and carefree way of life. But a sudden violent hemorrhage marked the beginning of another serious illness and brought an abrupt end to his present life style. It eventually necessitated Goethe's return to Frankfurt and entailed a nine month period of convalescence.

> The closer I came to my home town, the better I recalled in a rather disquieting way under what conditions, anticipations and hopes I had left home, and it was a very disheartening feeling that I was now returning like a castaway. (*D&W*, pt. 2, p. 370).

28 Bernhart Breitkopf set a number of verses written during that time to music and published them in Leipzig in 1770.

Again, much speculation has kept the scholars busy trying to determine the nature of this illness and the reasons for the author's efforts to obscure "the real causes." Again, for our purpose the "nature and real causes" of the illness are of little importance. It is, however, significant that Goethe used the incident again very effectively as a formal and thematic structural device. It takes place exactly in the middle of part II, book eight. Book eight consists of 48 1/3 pages and the event occurs on the second half of page 23. The remainder of the book is devoted to his return home, his convalescence. In book nine and ten Goethe completes his formal education in Strassburg, taking into account both his father's and his personal wishes. Thematically the illness marks the termination of another developmental phase on the poet's way to maturity. But it is more than just that. By his inclinations the young man had strayed again from the path outlined by his father. He had been sent to Leipzig to study law. He had failed—in a very Kantian sense—in his duties. Obviously, while the time had not been wasted as far as his personal development is concerned, it had been wasted as far as his "practical and utilitarian" advancement in this world—the bourgeois world—was concerned. And the father's concern was for both. A return to the recent point of departure seemed appropriate. If there was no cause for repentance, at least a re-orientation was in order.

It appears that every time Goethe returned to Frankfurt, whether from a short visit, from Leipzig, from Sesenheim, or even from Switzerland, he came home for a sort of hibernation or gestation period. He had sallied forth to Leipzig, arriving there muffled and buttoned up. He had—to use his metaphor of plant life—reached out, greened and blossomed. At the end of the allotted period, he folded up his petals and retreated to his origin, to his roots. Though in essence the same, his overall make-up had been greatly enhanced in quality by means of repeated cross-pollination. But this intellectual and spiritual refining process had weakened him physically. A rest period becomes imperative, complete seclusion and isolation from any new, disturbing, disquieting, or even exhilarating influences. This almost "dormant" stage is necessary in order to restore strength and vigour which alone can guarantee a renewed growing and blooming season.

Again and again we can observe this very elemental and most natural withdrawal movement. During these periods Goethe cuts himself off from any outside intercourse. It is a time for introspection, not in painful self-analysis, but a taking stock of his accomplishments, of his shortcomings. It is also a time to reappraise the family situation and his relationship with the various family members. His Leipzig experience had sharpened his perception and his intellect. He can evaluate his growth by comparing his letters written over a three-year period. He can smile about the pretentiousness of the sixteen-year-old trying to "educate" his younger sister. He had the leisure to re-evaluate some of his activities, comparing his father's and other people's judgment about one and the same thing. And he sees that maybe his father is not always right, is not the omnipotent person he always thought him to be.

> Time lasts indefinitely and every day is a vessel, into which one can pour many a thing, if one is intent on filling it up. (*D&W*, pt. 2, p. 381).

This is also a time for reappraisal and reconfirmation of his religious views, a time to take up previously read books and reread them with greater understanding and deeper insights. It is a time for gathering strength for new and greater endeavours.

The return from Leipzig is not his last one, neither is his illness which precipitated it, the last apocalyptic event. There are others and they follow basically the same pattern. The greatest ceasura, however, is reserved for the end of the work. It is Goethe's permanent departure from family and hometown to follow Countess Amalia and Crown Prince Konstantin to Weimar. In taking his decisive step despite his father's explicit disapproval, Goethe terminates his previous phase of material and emotional dependence on his family. This step does not mark, however, the end of his growth, for only death could halt the ever continuing evolution and development of this ever curious and active mind.[29]

29 The heightening and developing of man's natural abilities was one of Goethe's lifelong preoccupations. Two days before his death he wrote the following letter to Wilhelm von Humboldt: "Je früher der Mensch gewahr wird dass es ein Handwerk, dass es eine Kunst gibt, die ihm zur geregelten Steigerung seiner natürlichen Anlagen verhelfen, desto glücklicher ist er; was er auch von aussen empfange schadet seiner eingeborenen Individualität

The last part of the work, as indicated before, is marked by a definite change or neglect of artistic execution. While part three is still structured with extreme care and each apocalyptic event is used to highlight the termination of one clearly marked phase and to introduce the beginning of another, sections of part four–especially books 18-20–show considerable structural and stylistic neglect. Too often we have the impression of reading a rough draft, a preliminary sketching. From an excursion to Schwyz, for example, the poet attempts to describe the feelings of exuberation which he and an accompanying friend experienced, but concedes: "I would not know how to describe this condition, if it did not say in the diary: laughter and jubilation lasted till midnight" (*D&W*, pt. 4, p. 804). Not only are there visible difficulties in recreating emotions experienced almost six decades earlier (Goethe is eighty-one now), there is obvious artistic neglect:

> We climbed the Rigi; at seven-thirty we stood next to the God-Mother in the snow; afterwards to the chapel, past the convent, in the inn Oxen.

> Painted the chapel from the Oxen on the eighteenth Sunday, in the morning. At noon to the Kaltbad or to the Dreischwesterbrunnen. A quarter past two we had climbed the height; we found ourselves in clouds which was doubly disagreeable: it ruined the view and in the form of fog, drizzled down. (*D&W*, pt. 4, p. 804)

Clearly Goethe's interest in the "individuum" has been superseded by his need to muse about a great variety of present and past events. His observations center now more around historical events. In a letter to Wilhelm von Humboldt he concedes that he looks at himself more and more from a purely historical point of view.[30] Goethe at 81

nichts. Das beste Genie ist das, welches alles in sich aufnimmt sich alles zuzueignen weiss ohne dass es der eigentlichen Grundbestimmung, demjenigen, was man Charakter nennt, im mindesten Eintrag tue, vielmehr solches noch erst recht erhebe und durchaus nach Möglichkeit befähige. (Goethe, *Briefe*, op. cit., vol. IV, p. 480)

30 "Darf ich mich . . . in altem Zutrauen ausdrücken, so gesteh ich gern, dass in meinen hohen Jahren mir alles mehr und mehr historisch wird: ob etwas in der vergangenen Zeit, in fernen Reichen, oder mir ganz nah räumlich im Augenblick vorgeht, ist ganz eins, ja ich erscheine mir selbst immer mehr geschichtlich. . ." (Goethe, *Briefe, op. cit.*, p. 463).

must have found it difficult to take up the threads of this work almost two decades later. Many of the impressions of his youth which had lingered so vividly until 1813 might have been effaced by 1831. Already in part 1, book 2, he had remarked on the incapacity to speak with the "vividness (or richness) of childhood" (die Fülle der Kindheit) and he deplored this shortcoming again in part four:

> "On the whole," he tells us, "this present narration lacks in its entity the diffuse verbosity and richness of youth which, conscious of itself, does not know what to do with its strength and ability. (*D&W*, p. 786).

Goethe, as we have seen, had been interested in and fascinated by autobiographical writings from his early youth. And although he enveloped his entire work in an aura of serene tranquility and harmony —the two elements he incessantly strove for during his entire lifetime—he delineates very clearly the underlying problems of the autobiography, as well as the necessary elements for such a work:

> There are few biographies which can present a pure, tranquil and continued progress of the individuum. Our life, just as the entity in which we are contained is made up of freedom and necessity. Our desire is in an incomprehensible way a prophetic anticipation of that which we are going to do under all circumstances. But these circumstances take hold of us in their own way. The *what* is within us, the *how* rarely depends on us, and for the *why* we are supposed to enquire, and that is why we are directed quite rightly to the quia. (*D&W*, pt. 3, p. 524).

The creating artist succeeds in bringing all these elements together to form a unified whole, showing the *what*, the *how* and the *why*. In the end we see the man in his simplicity as well as in his complexity, but above all we understand quite thoroughly the *quia*.

In *Wilhelm Meister* (Book four) Goethe tells us:

> I admire the human being who knows what he wants, who, advancing incessantly, understands the means to his end, and who knows how to find and to handle them. . . . The greatest part of misfortune and that which is called evil in the world comes about only because men are too sloven about acquainting themselves accurately with their ends, and, when they have discovered them, fail to work seriously toward them.

Goethe at a relatively early time in his life established what he calls "man's ends." For him it meant an incessant striving toward moral, spiritual, and intellectual perfection. *Dichtung und Wahrheit* represents one phase towards this end.

The poet never was timid about letting the world know that he, Goethe, was a man of genius. Yet, though he took himself probably more seriously than any other of his contemporaries and though the protagonist of the autobiography is generally speaking the author himself, we find him rather frequently in the wings rather than in the foreground when great political events pass accross the stage of life. Totally disinterested in politics, he unfolds both the coronation and the French occupation before our eyes, conscious of the importance of such historic events. Though his participation in such events is primarily that of an onlooker, they nevertheless leave a deep and lasting imprint on his impressionable mind. The same holds true for countless encounters with outstanding and illustrious personalities in both the humanities and the sciences. They are shown with their achievements, but also with their human weaknesses, their greatness and foibles. Gratefully Goethe acknowledges his indebtedness to many a remarkable man who crossed his path, even though the full impact of their meeting might have shown itself only years later--maybe only at the time of the writing of *Dichtung und Wahrheit* itself. Young Goethe was in many of these encounters nothing more than an appendage, tolerated because of his curiosity, his genuine interest in almost any man's achievements and endeavours. At times we find him as a most humble disciple, enthralled by a great man's ideas and ideals, at others we frown at the arrogant, precocious youngster who permits himself evaluations and judgments of personalities and achievements which might be acceptable from Geheimrat Goethe's vantage point at age 60 or 80 but seem rather incongruous coming from a sixteen-year-old's mouth.

In most cases Goethe gives a description of the world around him, a commentary at times so intense that the author seems to forget he is writing his autobiography and lapses into the third person singular. He does not attempt to paint a picture of a model child, a studious young scholar, or even a model lover. We rather find him to be a quite average youngster of a rather typical bourgeois family, who feels more at ease with the working class child, who is easily impressed by this poetry-writing and fairy-tale telling friend Goethe.

162

We see the adolescent taking in all the sights and ventures of a basically carefree existence. With butterfly ease he seems to flutter and tumble from experience to experience, from one field of interest to another. But these stops are carefully calculated to coincide with Goethe's structural purpose of the work. Well aware of his poetic mission and of the didactic value of his autobiography, he solved for us the ultimate puzzle and shows us the *quia* of the existence of a genius. If for the sake of art some factual data had to be modified, omitted, or added, we will forgive him if we recall his ultimate artistic aim:

> The greatest obligation of every art is to evoke by means of illusion a more sublime reality, (*D&W*, p. 634).

Poetry for Goethe, as for Wordsworth, had become second nature. *Dichtung und Wahrheit* is the ultimate fusion of two principles: the poet and his art, forged into one inseparable and indivisible entity, the essence of the indefatigably creating artist. Goethe's as well as Wordsworth's autobiography is subjected to the same principle: art. "That wonderful reinterpretation (Umdeutung) of his youth," says Heinrich Meyer, "is only one of many possible poetic reflections of the real Goethe which, however, does not do justice to his essence (Wesen).[31] Nevertheless, this "reinterpretation" conveys exactly what Goethe set out to convey: the growth and life of a poet AS REFLECTED IN HIS AND THROUGH HIS WORKS. *Dichtung und Wahrheit* contributed probably more to the Goethe Myth, than any eulogy of the poet's most ardent admirers. It appears to be the very basis upon which Eckermann in turn erected his altar, on which the incense has been kept burning for amost two centuries. Only recently, have there been occasional attempts to clear the smoke in order to allow a clearer and better view at the real *Wesen* of Goethe, the man, whom we have problems discerning in *Dichtung und Wahrheit*. Both *Dichtung und Wahrheit* and J.-J. Rousseau's *Confessions*, though radically different in almost every respect, have one thing in common: each work presents its author to the world in a light most closely resembling the picture each man had of himself. Of necessity such a picture had to be in accordance with the respective philoso-

31 Heinrich Meyer, *op. cit.*, p. 594.

phy of life each man had espoused or at least attempted to espouse, and to which the writer, inherent in the man, had committed himself in numerous works. Under these circumstances it seems quite natural that each writer omitted--consciously or subconsciously--these aspects of his life and actions which did not coincide, or, worse, were in direct conflict with his philosophy. If we add in Goethe's case his artistic preoccupations (both with form and content) to the philosophical/pedagogical ones, we must concede that the autobiographical content of *Dichtung und Wahrheit* is the least important aspect of the work, that, in fact, it served primarily as a fulcrum for the reiteration of many of his previously expressed ideas and observations.

CHAPTER VI

A METHODOLOGICAL COMPARISON--CONCLUSION

In the preceding chapters we have seen how four influential writers used, enriched, and adapted the autobiography to their particular objectives. While Jean-Jacques Rousseau contributed to the autobiographical genre most decisively from the point of view of language, style, and syntax, his *Confessions* also inaugurated the era of a new man, extremely conscious and proud of his individuality, of his uniqueness. A new sensibility, a new and more profound self-consciousness permeate his entire work. The other three authors, making similar contributions to their respective national literature, subjected the autobiography to an even greater extent than Rousseau to their particular objectives whether literary and/or philosophical so that, in the end, the individual, the man, tends to disappear behind the artist-philosopher. Their autobiographies, as a consequence, are in many instances no longer a record of or testimony to the life they lived, but a poetically or philosophically transformed version of it. They deliberately flaunted the autobiographer's creed to "unfold in retrospect and in all sincerity the experiences and events which shaped his personality, his spiritual, and/or artistic development." Although their works represent a marked deviation from the genre, they neither superseded nor ousted the conventional autobiography. Despite a Rousseau, a Wordsworth, a De Quincey, and a Goethe, men continued to feel the urge to write about their life with no ulterior motive, no other objective except to review, to take stock, or simply to leave an account of their existence.

The full extent of the tremendous evolution within the autobiographical genre from circa 1770 to 1850 can best be seen by comparing and contrasting the previously discussed works with a conventional autobiography. In order to allow valid conclusions, such a work must have been written by a man whose life and preoccupations show a certain amount of similarities with the other four authors. Franz Grillparzer (1791-1872) is such a man. A methodological comparison will show the conventional autobiographer's approach to his work, his limitations, but also its advantages.

Reader and spectator alike are fascinated by the dramatic eloquence of every one of the characters brought to life on stage by Austria's foremost playwright, Franz Grillparzer. The intensity of their emotional struggles brought about by opposing polarities of interest, inclination and duty, emotions and reason, deeply touches any audience, reminding it of the ever-present human need to examine and resolve forever anew man's existential dilemmas and commitments. The scope and depth of these plays, their language, dynamic and overpowering, tender or entreating, rank Grillparzer among the greatest playwrights. Their performances in the German-speaking world enjoy continued acclaim and popularity, and their characters evoke today as much compassion and horror, love and contempt as they did during their first presentation at the Burgtheater in Vienna during Grillparzer's time.

In his works Grillparzer places his protagonist at a strategically important temporal and spatial spot where his personal commitment determines frequently not only his own individual fate, but the future course of history itself. The playwright, just like his creations, was born into such a time and such a place, when and where history was made. Vienna of the 1800's was second to no other European town in cultural and political activity and importance. The author was a contemporary of Emperor Franz, Prince Metternich and Napoleon, Beethoven and Schumann, Goethe and Tieck, Lord Byron and Dumas, to name only a few of the most famous personalities. He was acquainted with and befriended by most of these and countless more who were no less famous during their days. He knew some of the most famous as well as the most controversial men on the cultural and political scene. He witnessed Napoleon's victories and his defeat, the dissolution of the Holy Roman Empire of the German Nation and the decline of the powerful House of Hapsburg. He loved and was loved by some of the most beautiful and intelligent women in Vienna. His extensive travels took him through Germany, Italy, France, England, and Greece and he was a guest in the houses of countless illustrious personalities.

166

These, briefly, are some of the external circumstances of Grillparzer's life which undoubtedly played a rather active part in shaping his genius and his personality, and it is with considerable interest and anticipation that one turns to his autobiographical writings in order to see how the author, whose plays are singularly awe-inspiring and exciting in their quiet grandeur and impassioned eloquence, had incorporated all these events and experiences into his own life.

Grillparzer made three attempts at writing an autobiography. None was published during his lifetime, nor was any ever completed.[1] His first effort dates back to the year 1822, the second to 1834-1835, and the third and final one to 1853-1854. His first autobiographical attempt, he tells us, was prompted by Brockhaus' request, the publisher and book dealer, who had asked the author to furnish some data about his life for inclusion in the *Konversationslexikon.*[2] Parenthetically the author informs the reader immediately that he "shall do nothing of the kind." Nevertheless, this request prompted him to record before he completely forgets any details he may recall from his early youth.

This entire first autobiographical effort consists of five different recollections, each chronologically as well as thematically disconnected. Much like Edward Gibbon some thirty-five years before him, Grillparzer here is groping at half-forgotten incidents of long by-gone times. It is his search for traces of familiar faces and voices long since faded into oblivion. Though these recollections (covering a total of only four pages) are undoubtedly valuable in shedding some light on the writer's earliest and most dominating interests during childhood years, they are much too disconnected, and above all too limited in scope, to be considered anything but fragmentary sketches. The second attempt, written–like Abraham Lincoln's–in the third person singular, must be dismissed for the same reasons.

In 1848 the newly founded Akademie der Wissenschaften in Vienna asked its member, Franz Grillparzer, to furnish some data about his life. It was a routine procedure, because the *Akademie* used these

1   The greatest number of conventional autobiographies share this fate. Cellini's, Cardano's, Gibbon's, Grimm's, Stendhal's, are only a few examples where death terminated the author's work.

2   *The Konversationslexikon,* published by Brockhaus, was the forerunner of today's *Brockhaus Encyclopedia.*

lives in lieu of obituaries for its members. But the author delayed. The Akademie repeated its request four years later and again during the first days of 1853. It was only then that Grillparzer grudgingly consented. And like Goethe with his fictional letter, he assures his readers that it was not vanity or the desire for self-revelation or self-glorification which prompted him to take up his pen and to write about his life.

> The *Akademie* is asking me (now for the third time) to furnish for its almanac the circumstances surrounding my life, I shall try it, but I fear to go on rambling when the interest should start to wane. But then it can always be shortened later on.[3]

This is about as explicit and as condescending a statement as he can make without eliciting the wrath of the Akademie. He plainly tells his reader: I am not writing this by my own choice. In fact, I stalled as long as I could. The last sentence in particular emphasizes his attitude most succinctly. What he is saying, in fact, is: such a task can only be of temporary interest to me before it becomes too boring to concentrate on it, and I could not care less what will be done with this work once I get through with it. "Man kann ja aber später auch abkürzen." The impersonal pronoun "man" instead of "I" underlines this attitude already established with "when the interest should start to wane" (wenn sich das Interesse daran einstellen sollte).

Now one may be tempted to say: "this is all very nice and good, but what does it have to do with his autobiography? Why dwell on such trivia?" If we recall that each of the four previously discussed writers pursued a clearly identified objective *besides* the one of recording their lives, that, in fact, the changes they introduced were largely determined by these other objectives, then we can see why it is important to insist on the fact that Grillparzer had no compelling reason to deviate from the conventional autobiography. His work was to contain nothing but the unadultered truth about his life. An artistically transformed version would never do for him. At an earlier date he had discarded the thought of keeping a poetic diary for fear

3   Grillparzer, *Werke*, 2 vol., Tempel Klassiker, Berlin und Darmstadt, Der Tempel Verlag, ed. Paul Stapf, 1965. All references to Grillparzer's autobiography are to this edition, volume 2, and will be given in the text as follows (Autob. p. #). All translations are my own.

that "truth might suffer and the doors be opened wide for self-deception with the effort to give certain artistic form to the events of the day."[4] For him, it was to be one or the other, for reconciliation of life and art appeared utterly out of the question.

Grillparzer was sixty-two years old when he wrote his autobiography. He did not write it for pecuniary reasons. He was not in search of immortality. His literary work was sufficient guarantee for a spot on Mount Olympus. But, while he gave free rein to his imagination and fantasy in his poetic creations, while feelings and emotions there reached abysmal depths and soaring heights, his autobiography is a matter-of-fact account of his life in a matter-of-fact, politely conversational tone with occasional lapses into Viennese colloquialism. Description of family and friends, home and school, are stripped to the barest factual minimum. This becomes particularly apparent, when we contrast some of the experiences or events in his life with similar ones in the poetically transformed or elaborated works of a Goethe or a Rousseau.

A world of difference separates Goethe's elaborate, previously discussed, arrival in this world—with cosmos, hometown, friends and family assisting the event—from Grillparzer's statement: "I was born in Vienna on January 15, 1791" (Autob., p. 744). Rousseau and Goethe, in conformity with their objectives, had developed the father's portrait and shown his paternal role and influence throughout their formative years. Grillparzer's description of his father, rather short and to the point, conveys in a few sentences the father-son relationship:

> My father was an attorney, a strictly upright, reserved man. His business dealings and his natural taciturnity did not permit him to busy himself much with his children. He died before I had completed my eighteenth year and, since during the last years of his life, his sickness, the horrible war years and the domestic deterioration both entailed, only increased his taciturnity, I am unable to give to myself and to others an account of his inner nature. His outward behavior had something gruff and cold, he avoided all company, but was a passionate friend of nature. (Autob., p. 744).

4   Grillparzer, quoted in Hoff and Cermak, *Grillparzer--Versuch einer Pathographie*, Wien, Bergland Verlag, 1961, p. 28.

Grillparzer's language here has the dry, impersonal quality of the Austrian official that he was. It almost reads like a court deposition. The amount of information compressed into one sentence is truly amazing. Yet, all the facts are blatantly bare. We learn that the father's business dealings prevented him from spending time with his children. We wonder why— Were they out of town? Were they that exhausting? Did they demand an excessive amount of his time, of his attention? One single qualifying adjective could have clarified the situation. But such an adjective would have carried subjective rather than objective meanings, something the author is trying to avoid at all cost. The only instance where he permits himself any emotional display is in the expression "horrible war years'" But the adjective here must convey all the calamities and deprivations the Austrians suffered during the ravages of the Napoleonic invasions.

We have watched Goethe develop his love for the theater in an ascending line from his grandmother's gift (the puppet theater), the opportunity for daily theater visits (thanks to his grandfather's season pass), his readings of the great French playwrights, to his own productions. Grillparzer, whose life and preoccupations with the theater are intricately intertwined, recalls the first experience in the theater:

> I only remember that I was terribly bored and only one scene amused me, where the people were drinking chocolate in the gazebo and the dandy of the piece, rocking with his chair, fell, cup and all, backwards on the floor. (Autob., p. 751).

Surely, such a reaction from a future playwright seems shocking. Yet, isn't it precisely such a scene a ten-year-old would remember? It certainly seems much closer to the actual experience of such a boy than Goethe's professed interest in the polemics of French writers in the quarrel "*des Anciens et des Modernes*," or his and his sister's recitation of Klopstock's *Messias* at about the same age as Grillparzer's.

About his religion--or rather lack of it--Grillparzer has this to say:

> My church orientation was, by the way, not the least bit religious. My father grew up during Joseph's time and did not think too highly of spiritual exercises. The mother went to mass every Sunday, with the servant carrying her prayer book behind her; we children never went to church. (Autob., p. 751).

170

Goethe never went to church. Neither did Wordsworth in his *Prelude*. Yet, both of these men spend considerable thought on the question of religion and each one arrived in due time at a very personal relationship with his Creator. Obviously such a quest involved in many instances years of soul-searching, and their works reflect it. Even De Quincey's dreams were at times transfigured with the hope and life emanating from an eternal God.[5] No apocalyptic experience prompted Grillparzer to give up his religion or to turn his back on the priest who had come to give him the sacraments. His father "wuchs auf zu Josefs Zeiten" and "hielt nichts von Andachtsübungen." The reader, of course, is supposed to know that during this time certain libertine ideas, imported from France, prevailed in this otherwise solidly Catholic country. And the mother's piety, apparent here and there in the autobiography, obviously did not impress or influence the children.

The contrast is just as striking when we look at Grillparzer's period of higher education.

> Now comes a dreary, desolate time [eine wüste, trübe Zeit] which fortunately lasted only a year. I changed over to the university. Thoughts about academic freedom which affect everybody, befell me stronger than anybody else. Unfortunately our professors were of the sort that only a habit of diligence—in which I did not believe—could encourage continuation of it. (Autob., p. 762).

The "dreariness" of this experience becomes all the more apparent if we compare it to Wordsworth's or Goethe's poetically transformed accounts of their university experiences. Neither one seems to have been an exemplary student. Yet, while they may not have pursued their studies with optimal diligence, the former two profited immeasurably as far as their personal enrichment was concerned. They, too, observed and expressed the negative aspects of formal education (just as Goethe had hinted many times at, what he considered, his father's shortcomings), but the context in which the criticism is shown, the language—syntax and diction—subordinate the negative to the positive aspects. Grillparzer's style is—to say the least—at times

---

5   cf. J.H. Miller, *The Disappearance of God*, New York, Schocken Books, 1965.

terribly awkward (psychologists would probably consider it a demonstration of his reluctance to talk about himself). Only the passages dealing with his literary endeavours become more animated and rythmically fluent. His prose never becomes impassioned. His paranoia and his deep-seated pessimism prevented him from seeing any joy even in his earliest years, which might have inspired him (as it did Rousseau) to record some emotional reaction.

As we read Grillparzer's autobiography we find countless similarities in his life with the other four authors. By temperament he was probably closest to Rousseau. It would take a separate study to contrast all of them with similar experiences described in the works of Goethe, Wordsworth, or Rousseau. Contrary to these, however, he presents his without ornament. He was basically a sober man whose passions, as we can see in his autobiography, were sublimated in his plays, i.e., the world of fiction he created there. His autobiography is the sincere effort to record his past life.[6] He does not attribute particular significance to any one influence, nor any one experience. He sees his life filled with fleeting faces whether in Vienna, Paris, Rome or London with which he feels no communion, no brotherhood. Like Goethe he had read Rousseau's *Confessions*, he had visited Rome and Naples, but nowhere do we find a word, a hint, that such things impressed him in any way. Rousseau's agonizing attempt to show the workings of his heart, the vibrations of his soul, to portray the complexity of his emotions and his feelings which he thought so fundamentally different from any other man, in a language so radically different from contemporary prose writings, none of these influenced Grillparzer. He had read Goethe's *Dichtung und Wahrheit* with its richness of descriptive detail, its depiction of the poet's growth and development, its fascinating character portraits, but not a single passage in Grillparzer's autobiography shows the slightest trace of influence. But his work reflects its author's character more unmistakably than Rousseau's or Goethe's. Grillparzer's gruff, misanthrophic, frequently spiteful personality is best characterized by his dry, surly,

6   Only in one instance did he deviate from truth. He did not find his mother dead from a stroke upright behind her bed. She had hanged herself. Neither did he mention any one of his love affairs for, as he pointed out, these secrets were not his own to reveal.

official prose, just as Rousseau's temperament is best shown by his languishing, elegiac style.

The great advantage of such a conventional autobiography is, of course, that the reader can come to his own conclusion about the life and the character of the author. He is not told what to think and his emotions are not manipulated--as in the case of Rousseau. He does not have to wonder perpetually whether the author tells his life or is giving free rein to his fancy. In Grillparzer's autobiography is no trace of self-glorification, only here and there a show of overwhelming vanity.

There are obvious limitations to such a work. Most conventional confessions suffer from a lack of literary merit. Only a very limited number of readers (those who have a particular interest in the author), would be attracted to buy it, unless its very title promises some scandalous revelations to make it palatable for a larger group of readers. In any event, such works rarely stand the test of time. And in this respect Grillparzer's autobiography is a typical example. His life, as we find it in the work, cannot serve as an inspiration for emulation; it does not show us generally applicable truths nor revelations; there is no grappling with existential problems, no coming to terms with life. Crucial historical events, acquaintances with great personalities, births and deaths of family members and friends, are--if mentioned at all--described with so much neglect and banality, so much personal rancor as to rob them of any value even for the scholar. The man Grillparzer we find in the autobiography seems to have little or no relation to the individual who wrote such plays as *Das goldene Vliess* or *Des Meeres und der Liebe Wellen* or who would be a composite of the historical reality as outlined on page 166.

Of course, not all conventional autobiographies reflect such an overwhelming amount of egocentricity. Leigh Hunt's, for example, is a fascinating study of the contemporary scene, the joys and problems of the author's life, the friendships he cultivated. It will probably hold the interest of many a scholar for decades to come. But Leigh Hunt is rather the exception than the rule. Also, the interest in his work is, in a not inconsiderable measure, due to the fact that he was associated with the Romantic movement and the Romantic poets, and his work, in addition to telling the story of his life, sheds considerable light on these relationships. Every scholar interested in Shelley or Byron will inevitably turn to Leigh Hunt's autobiography in hopes of better understanding them with the help of Hunt's testimony.

The conventional autobiography--as we have seen-was neither affected nor superseded by the changes introduced by Rousseau, Wordsworth, De Quincey, and Goethe. Depending on the skill of its author, his disposition, and his background, it continues to interest readers because it remains at all times a genuine unadultered portrait of an individual human being and--depending on his nature--his involvement in the contemporary scene.

It is important to remember that the changes within the autobiographical genre were not instituted by any one of the hundreds of autobiographers who recorded their lives during these decades in any language and any country. Rousseau, Wordsworth, Goethe, and De Quincey were extraordinary men. Their lives from their earliest youth had been intricately connected with literature, especially the literature reflective of mankind's history, hopes, and aspirations. Rousseau, Wordsworth, and Goethe had high literary ambitions. Each was well aware that lasting fame is only bestowed on those who blaze a new trail, that the laurels are never carried off by *Epigonen*. Rousseau, Wordsworth, Goethe, and, by coincidence more than by design, De Quincey succeeded in blazing this trail. Rousseau achieved distinction and fame internationally, Wordsworth in the English speaking and Goethe in the German speaking world, De Quincey in both in England and in France. Goethe's *Dichtung und Wahrheit* probably produced less resonance than any of the other works. The reasons are very obvious. The poet tells the reader "every thing I ever wrote was a fragment of a confession, this little book is merely an attempt to complete it." Both, the work's underlying thematic structure and his views on man and the world had already found expression in countless smaller and larger works, but most succinctly in his *Wilhelm Meister*, so that his *Dichtung und Wahrheit* did not contain anything resembling the revolutionary revelations found in the other three works.

We have seen Rousseau tell his reader about the uniqueness of his endeavour. It is unique because the individual whose life he describes is unique. It was pointed out before that his work is reflective of a new man, modern man, caught in a most decisive identity crisis. Rousseau's problems and agonies are representative of the innumerable men and women thrust forth into a hostile world devoid of any solidly grounded pole from which they could derive a sense of orientation and security. No longer does man feel solidly anchored and emotionally secure within a hermetically closed society held together by century-old religious and historical traditions. Rather, he finds himself surrounded by constant flux, the ties cut from family, religion, tradition, and history, fluttering loosely and irresolutely in whichever direction progress and science would blow him. Rousseau was the first to leave a record, his record, representative of countless men and women who shared similar emotions, similar fates. As a fifteen-year-old youngster he had irrevocably severed all strings with family, hometown, country, and even his religion and set himself adrift in a world with which he was not equipped to cope. All his life he was acutely and painfully aware of his isolation and alienation and, after having probed deeply within himself and not having found any answers for his miseries, he blames man and the world for it. His agonizing longing for roots, security, and warmth is nowhere more apparent than in his futile wish that seems to emanate from the very bottom of his heart: "Ah, had I only stayed in my home town, had I only become a watchmaker!" Then, he feels, he would have been surrounded by family and friends, he would have been a useful member of the Genevan society, be it ever so humble. This is the picture of ultimate peace and tranquility for the haunted, isolated, alienated, and unhappy individual.

Wordsworth, by the very circumstances of his life, had experienced similar feelings, just as intensely, just as painfully. But being of different temperament, of a different nature than Rousseau, he could not content himself with the exposition of such an identity crisis. Like Goethe he believed in the perfectability of mankind. Deceived and disappointed by mankind's so-called progress, disillusioned with the massive effort to cure social injustice and ameliorate man's lot, he sought and found meaning and purpose within himself, security and emotional stability in his intercourse with Nature, fulfillment in his self-imposed missionary role. *The Prelude* is at once the record of Wordsworth's identity crisis, but at the same time the testimony to his ability to overcome it. He too had searched within himself, and he, too, had discovered his inability to understand and to solve the existential enigma with his own powers. In all the tumultuous flux and reflux he experiences, he finds Nature the only permanently fixed reality. For him it becomes the stable pole which enables him to orient and reorient himself. In it, he again achieves the sense of wholeness which he had lost. Not the identity crisis, but the capability and the means to overcome it, were Wordsworth's great contributions.

The situation with De Quincey is considerably more complex. We have seen that his envisioned work had absolutely nothing in common with the autobiographical work which he produced. His aspirations—according to the author—lay in the field of philosophy and mathematics. The fact that his *Confessions* scored almost overnight sensational success was due more to the sensational nature of its disclosures than to generally valid observations and applicable truths. Yet, in more than one way, De Quincey is another representative of the disoriented, alienated man so prevalent in our society ever since the 1800s. He, too, was in search of direction when he happened upon his panacea for all his physical and spiritual woes, opium. De Quincey tells us later in the revised *Confessions* (1856) that it was not pain, but misery, not "casual overcasting of sunshine, but bland desolation; not gloom, but settled and abiding darkness" which made him reach again and again for his laudanum decanter.[7] Incapable of coming to terms with contemporary society and himself, De Quincey –like Rousseau before him–took refuge in his dreams. But Rousseau spun his dream webs out of the fond memories of bygone days, while De Quincey abandoned himself to the enchanting pleasures of his opium dreams. Yet, although he speaks abundantly about the delights and the grandeur of his early dreams, i.e., before his opium excesses, the examples of the dreams he provides for the reader are, in striking contrast to Rousseau's, invariably alarming and distressing

---

7   In view of De Quincey's own statement it seems inconceivable that E. Sackville-West can make a statement such as this: "De Quincey, as I have tried to make clear, took opium primarily as a painkiller" *op. cit.*, p. 238.

in character.

We have seen that only years after the original publication of the *Confessions* did De Quincey become aware of the importance of his dreams. It is doubtful, he ever realized that his experiences as related in the *Confessions* actually represented a continuation of a quest for self-understanding started by Rousseau and carried on by Wordsworth. Rousseau had explored his heart and his soul, Wordsworth the development of his mind, the former simply by folding back within himself, the latter by immersing himself in Nature. But De Quincey, with the help of opium, probed the human mind more thoroughly than it had ever been probed before. Later in the century, Balzac's imagination brought to life the whole "comedie humaine," Victor Hugo "La legende des siècles." But De Quincey, whose imaginative faculty was supposedly limited,[8] relived with the help of opium the entire history of mankind. He could experience simultaneously Rousseau's heavenly state of bliss at Les Charmettes, Wordsworth's Mount Snowden, E.T.A. Hoffmann's musical ecstacies, Poe's abysmal terrors and abject horrors. His mind, by the power of opium, was laid bare and all the experiences ever impressed upon it surged forth unhampered, uncontrolled. All elements foreign, strange, and horrifying converged upon this quiet and sedate man, who is so conscious of his "Englishness" of his social class, his traditions and mode of life, to whom any deviation from these standards appears horrifying, barbarous. To be sure, he has a certain intellectual curiosity about things Eastern, or African, exotic and strange, but to be directly confronted by them in his dreams brought about not only "moral and spiritual terrors" but "physical horror" as well (*Conf.*, p. 246). Davis calls De Quincey's opium experiences his effort to become "homme-dieu."[9] I do not believe the Opium-Eater had such intentions. Nowhere does the author indicate such aspirations.

It is tempting to speculate today on De Quincey's "real" motives, especially in view of the tremendous medical discoveries (particularly in the field of psychology) during the course of this century. It is

8   cf. René Wellek, "De Quincey's Status in the History of Ideas," *Philological Quarterly*, XXIII, 1944, pp. 248-272.

9   Hugh S. Davis, *Thomas De Quincey*, London, Longmans, Green & Co. 1964.

even more tempting to exaggerate the importance he attributed to his dreams. H. Davis writes:

> It must not be forgotten that he [De Quincey] was not concerned with dream writing for its own sake. It was no more, and no less, than the special material on which he founded his study of the growth of the human spirit . . . De Quincey is too often read for the sake of his purpler passages, without regard for the exploration of which they are merely a part.[10]

And J.H. Miller, considering the death of De Quincey's sister as the central event of the *Confessions*, tells us that the author's self-awareness is generated by "the sudden revelation that all is lost" that for him conscious life begins at the moment when life (i.e., Elizabeth's life) is finished.[11] We have, however, seen that the sister's death did not even figure in the original *Confessions,* that the vocabulary, symbolism, and imagery used in this particular scene in the *Suspiria*, had been identical with those related to a very general observation on life and death in the 1821-1822 *Confessions.* Furthermore, in preparing the revised work for publication, De Quincey indicates nowhere that he has added forgotten or previously overlooked events and experiences *important to the understanding of his life.* His preoccupations during his revisions are almost exclusively of a literary nature, i.e., style, syntax, effect on the reader, etc. He acknowledges that the work "had originally been written hastily" (Rev. *Conf.*, p. 100) that "the main narrative should naturally have moved through a succession of secondary incidents; and with leisure for recalling these, it might have been greatly inspirited." The writer knows he is telling a story and in order to retain his reader's interest, the story must move at a reasonable speed, show highlights and suspense, i.e., it must be entertaining. And among the "secondary incidents" he supplies is the dramatically well developed death of his sister. But it appears that, rather than attributing to it special significance for De Quincey's de-

10 Hugh S. Davis, *Thomas De Quincey, op. cit.*, p. 33 [brackets added].

11 J.H. Miller, *The Disappearance of God, op. cit.*, p. 12. D. Grant is belaboring the same fallacy when he tells his readers: "The deaths of his sister and of his father . . .dominate the opening of the work and carry us immediately into the mysterious intellectual solitudes of his imagination" *Some British Romantics*, ed. Logan, Jordan & Frye, Columbus, Ohio State University Press, 1966, p. 157.

velopment, it should be regarded as one of his fictional opium dreams of later years.

De Quincey seems to have lived with his dreams much in the manner Rousseau and Grillparzer lived with their sicknesses. Just as an ailing man is aware of the various dimensions of physical sufferings his sickness inflicts upon him, so De Quincey is aware of the greater perceptual dimensions his dreams added to his consciousness. In the course of his addiction, they became more and more a part of his life, and, as we have seen, he tended to see his life--past and present--especially in later years more and more through his dreams and visions. Rousseau and Wordsworth had deliberately sought an answer to the existential mystery as they experienced it. De Quincey, by a strange twist of circumstances, perceived the unfathomable immensity of this mystery. With unprecedented clarity he describes its abysmal dimension and horrifying aspects as he had experienced it in his dreams. Kenneth Johnston tells us "it is hard to tell when ordinary sight transmutes into vision in Wordsworth's poetry--but this difficulty is, as much as anything else, the very essence of his genius."[12] With De Quincey we can say that in any of his autobiographical works, written after the original *Confessions*, it is hard to tell when ordinary life is being transmuted by his opium dreams and visions. Surely the inclusion of the very dramatic description of his sister's death and his vision in Shrewbury make for more entertaining and more varied reading. Above all they convey upon the protagonist a quasi-mystical dimension which, in reality, he did not have, at least not at that time of his life. It is this aspect of his work that brings us right back to the heart of this study.

Each one of the four authors recorded in his work highly personal experiences of his life. In each work we watch the author's often agonizing efforts to come to terms with a world and a society from which he feels by nature or circumstances alienated. Wordsworth and Goethe succeed in resolving their problems in their works admirably well. De Quincey's work does not have the literary breadth or the philosophical depth of either work. His panacea turns out to be a

---

12 Kenneth R. Johnston, "The Idiom of Vision," in *New Perspectives on Coleridge and Wordsworth*, ed. Geoffrey H. Hartmann, New York and London, Columbia University Press, 1972, p. 3.

curse more than a means of salvation. Wordsworth's poetic confirmation and Goethe's ceaseless striving enabled them to overcome their existential crisis, De Quincey's dreams failed to do so. Yet, as we have seen, these authors were not merely concerned with the recording of their life's experiences. Each one pursued clearly designed objectives and their autobiographical data were submitted to these objectives.

Rousseau–as we have seen--has made the most decisive contributions to the genre. He has enlivened, rejuvenated the autobiography. Nevertheless, he transgressed against the foremost prerequisite of any autobiography: sincerity. By professing to tell it all, the good as well as the evil in his life, he attempted something which had no precedent and which has not found any imitators. People have made partial confessions giving one or the other aspect in their lives more detailed attention and skipping over others. But Rousseau started to probe into the remotest feelings and inclinations of the six-year-old with the same thoroughness with which he dissected the virtues and vices of the forty-year-old. The phenomenal amount of details and trivia he recalls is awe-inspiring, and the skill with which he submits this to his overall purpose, his justification, is truly remarkable. Rousseau fulfills all the other prerequisites of a conventional autobiographer. He writes in retrospect and evaluates the experiences which he feels contributed to his development and his growth.[13] His work covers a substantial number of years and yet, because of the lucidity with which he set out to write this work, because of his continued insistence on the need for absolute sincerity, we must accuse him of having deliberately and wilfully violated the autobiographer's creed.

Wordsworth's transgressions were of an even greater consequence. Rousseau speaking of the autobiographers had said: "the most sincere are truthful more or less in what they say, but they lie in their reticences, and what they do not confess changes so much what they make a pretense of avowing that, by reason of recounting only one part of the truth, they tell us nothing." And Wordsworth certainly falls into this category. Too many important incidents such as the Annette-affair, his marriage, the birth of his children, and countless

13 Rousseau, *op. cit.*, p. 1149.

180

other events were omitted from the autobiography because they would have hampered the artistic structure of the work or because they were ill-suited to the thematic development of *The Prelude*. The autobiographical content in Wordsworth's case is not only subjected to one objective as with Rousseau, but to three. Wordsworth put to practice Goethe's axiom that "A fact of our life is not valid inasfar as it is factual, but inasfar as it has some meaning to it," by omitting all experiences which fail to support and further his thematic structure. But the *Prelude*--intended to be a part of Wordsworth's monument--exemplifies the poet's own concepts about autobiography: "Truth is not here . . . to be sought without scruple, and promulgated for its own sake, upon the mere chance of its being serviceable; but only for obviously justifying purposes, moral and intellectual." We have examined in Chapter III his justifying purposes and their effect upon the autobiographical content.

If Rousseau had immeasurably enriched the autobiography with his contributions, Wordsworth, making use of many of the newly introduced elements, undertook the unheard-of venture of basing, what he hoped to be, his poetical/philosophical masterpiece on the experiences of his own life. Because of the transgressions necessitated by his complex objectives, *The Prelude* constitutes a definite branching off the conventional autobiography. With *Dichtung und Wahrheit*, where the fictional aspect of the work is clearly underlined, *The Prelude* leads directly to such works as Rilke's *Notebooks of Malte Brigge*, Proust's *Remembrance of Things Past*, Mann's *Buddenbrooks* and *Tonio Kroger*, Joyce's *Portrait of the Artist*, and myriads more.[14] It seems, in fact, the autobiographical novel has become one of the most favored vehicles for expression for many of our twentieth-century writers. Maybe because of the ready availability of the subject matter, maybe--as Heinrich Meyer seems to suggest--because many modern writers don't have the necessary amount of imagination to develop a solid, substantial plot.

---

14 "Wordsworth's effect on the novelists, especially George Eliot," John Speirs tells us "seems to me to have been the most pervasive and profound. Wordsworth himself could have never been a novelist. . . . He did have insights as a poet which revealed new possibilities for the novelists." John Speirs, *Poetry Towards Novel*, London, Faber and Faber, 1971, p. 283.

De Quincey's objectives were considerably less complex, and his original *Confessions*, despite its strange and "unearthly" experiences, is easily accommodated within the conventional autobiography. The situation, however, changes radically and its position becomes highly questionable when he writes his sequel *Suspiria de Profundis* and revises his *Confessions*. For now his life--deliberately or subconsciously, we have no way of knowing--is being relived through his opium dreams. Is it still fact or does it approach fiction under these circumstances? De Quincey--we have seen--set out to write his autobiography and not a literary masterpiece. The special emphasis, of course, was to be on his most unique opium experiences. Like Montaigne, like Wordsworth, he wrote about what he knew best, his life. And as with Rousseau's and Wordsworth's works, the literary quality of his autobiography was far superior to anything he had ever written, or was ever going to write. But because of the "unreal" quality of the dreams, their fantasia-like impact, De Quincey finds his imitators not only among the French Symbolists, but also in works of fiction like Hogg's *Confessions of a Justified Sinner*, or Flaubert's *Tentation de Saint Antoine*, where every connection with the autobiography has been severed.

This study of five representative autobiographical works between 1770 and 1850 and the isolation of some of the elements which led to considerable evolution and eventual division of the autobiographical genre, does not solve the genre's initial dilemma. Rather, it has underlined the need for clearer distinction and better classification among the vast and diversified production of autobiographical and pseudo-autobiographical writings. More specific criteria must be applied by literary critics to these works in order to prevent the indiscriminate relegation of any and everything written in the first person singular to the now all but meaningless category of autobiographical writings.

BIBLIOGRAPHY

ALLOTT, Miriam, ed. *Novelists on the Novel*, New York: Columbia University Press, 1959.

ASCHENBRENNER, Karl and ISENBERG, Arnold. *Aesthetic Theories*, Englewood Cliffs, New Jersey: Prentice Hall, Inc., 1965.

AUERBACH, Erich. *Mimesis: The Representation of Reality in Western Literature*, tr. Willard R. Trask, Princeton, New Jersey: Princeton University Press, 1953.

AUGUSTINE, Saint. *The Confessions of . . .*, tr. E. B. Pusey, New York: Random House, Inc., The Modern Library, 1949.

Autobiography, Masterpieces of, ed. Iles George, Garden City, New York: Doubleday, Page & Company, 1926.

AXTHELM, Peter M. *The Modern Confessional Novel*, New Haven and London: Yale University Press, 1967.

BALL, Patricia M. *The Central Self*, Bristol: The Athelone Press, 1968.

BARZUN, Jacques. *Classic, Romantic and Modern*, Garden City, New York: Doubleday, 1961.

BATE, W. J. *From Classic to Romantic: Premises of Taste in Eighteenth Century England*, Cambridge, Mass.: Harvard University Press, 1946.

-.- *Criticism: The Major Texts*, New York: Harcourt Brace & Co., 1952.

BATES, E. S. *Inside Out: Introduction to Autobiography*, New York: Sheridon House, 1937.

BATESON, F. W. *Wordsworth—A Re-Interpretation*, New York and London: Longman, Green and Co., 1954.

BAUGH, A. C., ed. *A Literary History of England*, New York: Appleton-Century-Crofts, 1948.

BEEBE, Maurice. *Ivory Towers and Sacred Founts*, New York: University Press, 1964.

BELAVAL, Yvon. *Le Souci de sincerité*, Paris: Gallimard, 1944.

BENZINGER, James. *Images of Eternity: Studies in the Poetry of Religious Vision from Wordsworth to T. S. Eliot*, Carbondale: Southern Illinois University Press, 1962.

BEYER-FRÖHLICH, Marianne. *Höhe und Krise der Aufklärung*, Reihe deutscher Selbstzeugnisse, Leipzig: Verlag Philipp Reclam jun., 1934.

- . - *Pietismus und Rationalismus*, Reihe deutscher Selbstzeugnisse in 10 Bänden, Leipzig: Verlag Philipp Reclam jun., 1933.

BLACK, Frank G. *The Epistolary Novel in the Late Eighteenth Century*, Eugene: University of Oregon, 1940.

BLANCHARD, W. H. *Rousseau and the Spirit of Revolt*, Ann Arbor: University of Michigan Press, 1967.

BOCKMANN, Paul, ed. *Stil- und Formprobleme in der Literatur*, Heidelberg: Henry Remak, 1959.

BONNER, Willard H. *De Quincey at Work: As Seen in 130 New and Newly Edited Letters*, Buffalo: Airport Publisher, 1936.

BOOTH, Wayne E. *The Rhetoric of Fiction*, Chicago and London: University of Chicago Press, 1961.

BOSTETTER, E. E. *The Romantic Ventriloquists: Wordsworth, Coleridge, Keats, Shelley, Byron*, Seattle: University of Washington Press, 1963.

BRAND, C. P. *Main Currents in Nineteenth Century Literature*, 6 vol., New York: Russel & Russel, 1872-1890.

BRENTANO, Franz. *Grundzüge der Ästhetik*, Bern: A. Francke Verlags-AG., 1959.

BROWN, Robeson. *The Autobiography*, London: Cresset Press, 1909.

BRUNETIÈRE, Ferdinand. *L'évolution des genres littéraires*, Paris: Editions Mondiales, 1934.

BUTLER of Saffron Walden, *The Difficult Art of Autobiography*, Oxford: At the Clarendon Press, 1968.

CELLINI, Benvenuto. *Autobiography*, tr. J. Addington Symonds, Roslyn: Black's Readers Service Company, 1972.

COLLET, Dorothy. *Writing of Modern Confession Story*, Boston: The Writer, Inc., 1951.

COLUM, Mary. *From These Roots, The Ideas That Have Made Modern Literature*, New York: Scribners, 1938.

COURCELLE, Pierre. *Les Confessions de Saint Augustine dans la tradition littéraire*, Paris: Etudes Augustiniennes, 1963.

CROCKER, Lester G. *Jean-Jacques Rousseau: The Prophetic Voice*, 2 vol., New York: The Macmillan Company, 1973.

CROSS, Wilbur L. *Development of the English Novel*, New York: The Macmillan Company, 1911.

DAICHES, David. *A Critical History of English Literature*, 2nd ed., London: Secker and Warburg, 1960.

DAVIS, Hugh S. *Thomas De Quincey*, London: Longmans, Green & Co., 1964.

DEFOUR-VERNES, Louis. *Recherches sur J.-J. Rousseau et sa parenté*, Génève: 1878.

DE QUINCEY, Thomas. *The Collected Writings of . . .*, ed. David Masson, 14 vol., Edinburgh: Adam and Charles Black, 1889.

- . - *Confessions of an English Opium-Eater*, ed. Malcolm Elwin, London: Macdonald & Co., Ltd. 1956.

- . - *A Diary of . . .*, ed. Horace A. Eaton, London: Noel Douglas, n.d.

DOUGLAS, W. W. *Wordsworth: The Construction of a Personality*, Kent: Kent State University Press, 1968.

DROMMARD, Gabriel. *Les Mensonges et la vie intérieure*, Paris: Alcan, 1910.

DYSON, H. V. D. and BUTT, John. *Augustans and Romantics 1689-1830*, rev. ed., London: Cresset Press, 1950.

EATON, Horace A. *Thomas De Quincey*, New York: Oxford University Press, 1936.

EBNER-ESCHENBACH, Marie von. *Meine Erinnerungen an Grillparzer*, Wien: Bergland-Verlag, 1955.

ECKERMANN, Joh. Peter. *Gespräche mit Goethe*, 2 vol, Berlin: Deutsche Bibliothek, n.d.

ELTON, Oliver. *A Survey of English Literature 1780-1880*, 2 vol., London: E. Arnold, 1912-1920.

FERNANDEZ, Ramon. *L'autobiographie et le roman*, Paris: Messages, 1926.

FISCHER-LAMBERG, Hanna. *Der junge Goethe*, Neu bearbeitete Ausgabe, 5 vol., Berlin: Walter de Gruyter & Co., 1963.

FISKE, Charles. *The Confessions of a Puzzled Parson*, Freeport: Books for Libraries Press, 1968.

FOGLE, Stephen F. *Leigh Hunt's Autobiography*, Gainsville: University of Florida Monographs, 1959.

FRIEDENTHAL, Richard. *Goethe: His Life and Times*, Cleveland: The World Publishing Company, 1963.

FRYE, Northrop. *Anatomy of Criticism*, Princeton: Princeton University Press, 1957.

- . - *A Study of English Romanticism*, New York: Random House, 1968.

GIBBON, Edward. *Memoirs of my Life*, ed. G. A. Bonnard, New York: Funk & Wagnalls, 1969.

GINGERICH, S. F. *Essays in the Romantic Poets*. New York: Macmillan, 1924.

GIRARD, René. *Deceit, Desire and the Novel*, tr. Yvonne Freccero, Baltimore: The Johns Hopkins Press, 1965.

GLASER, LEHMANN and LUBOS. *Wege der Deutschen Literatur*, Frankfurt: Verlag Ullstein, GmbH., 1961.

GOETHE, Johann Wolfgang von. *Briefe* (Hamburger Ausgabe), 4 vol, ed. Karl R. Mandelkow, Hamburg: Christian Wegner Verlag, 1967.

GOETHE, Johann Wolfgang von . . . *erzählt sein Leben*, ed. H. E. Gerlach and O. Hermann, Frankfurt/M.: Fischer Bücherei, 1956.

- . - *The Autobiography of . . .*, tr. John Oxenford, London: Bell & Daldy, 1871.

- . - *Autobiography*, Bicentennial Edition, tr. R. O. Moon, Washington: Washington Affairs Press, 1949.

- . - *Poetry and Truth*, tr. Minna S. Smith, London: G. Bell and Sons, 1908.

- . - *Truth and Fiction--Relating to My Life*, tr. John Oxenford, New York: Anthological Society, 1901.

- . - *Truth and Poetry*, tr. A. Morrison, London: G. Bell and Sons, 1874.

- . - *Werke*, 36 vol., Stuttgart: Gotta'sche Jubiläumsausgabe, 1882.

- . - *Werke, Dichtung und Wahrheit*, vol. VIII, Zürich, Artemis Verlags-AG., 1972.

GOLDMAN, Albert. *The Mine and the Mint*, Carbondale and Edwardsville: Southern Illinois University Press, 1965.

GREEN, F. C. *Jean-Jacques Rousseau*, Cambridge: Harvard University Press, 1955.

Grillparzer Forum, ed. Elisabeth Schmitz-Mayr-Harting, Wien: Österreichischer Bundesverlag für Unterricht, Wissenschaft und Kunst, 1965.

GRILLPARZER, Franz. *Werke*, 2 vol, ed. Paul Stapf, Berlin: Der Tempelverlag, 1965.

GRIMSLEY, Ronald. *Rousseau and the Religious Quest*, Oxford: Clarendon Press, 1968.

GUEHÉNNO, Jean. *Jean-Jacques Rousseau*, 2 vol., tr. J. and D. Weightman, London: Routledge & Kegan Paul, 1966.

HAMMER, Carl. *Goethe and Rousseau: Resonances of the Mind*, Lexington: The University Press of Kentucky, 1973.

HARTMAN, Geoffrey H., ed. *New Perspectives on Coleridge and Wordsworth*, New York and London: Columbia University Press, 1972.

HARTMAN, Geoffrey H., ed. *Wordsworth's Poetry 1787-1814*, New Haven: Yale University Press, 1964.

HARPER, George Mclean. *William Wordsworth*, London: John Murray, 1929.

HAVENS, Raymond D. *The Mind of a Poet: The Prelude*, Baltimore: The Johns Hopkins Press, 1941.

HAZLITT, William. *Liber Amoris & Dramatic Criticisms*, London: Peter Nevill Ltd., 1948.

HELBIG, G., ed. *Franz Grillparzer: Sein Leben und Schaffen in Selbstzeugnissen*, Leipzig: Koehler und Amelang, 1957.

HERNARDI, Paul. *Beyond Genre: New Directions in Literary Classifications*, Ithaca and London: Cornell University Press, 1972.

HOFF, Hans and CERMAK, Ida. *Grillparzer–Versuch einer Pathologie*, Wien: Berland Verlag, 1961.

HOGG, James. *Private Memoirs and Confessions of a Justified Sinner*, London: Oxford University Press, 1969.

JAPP, Alexander. *Thomas De Quincey: His Life and Writings:* With Unpublished Correspondence, London: J. Hogg, 1890.

JOHNSON, Edgar. *One Mighty Torrent*, New York: The Macmillan Company, 1955.

JONES, John. *The Egotistical Sublime*, London: Chatto and Windus, 1970.

JORDAN, J. E. *De Quincey and Wordsworth: A Biography of a Relationship*, Berkeley and Los Angeles: University of California Press, 1962.

KAPLAN, Louis. *Bibliography of American Autobiographies* Madison: University of Wisconsin Press, 1961.

KAYSER, Wolfgang J. *Die Entstehung des modernen Romans*, 4th ed., Stuttgart: J. B. Metzlersche Verlagsbuchhandlung, 1963.

KILLY, Walter. *Wirklichkeit und Kunstcharakter*, München: C. H. Beck'sche Verlagsbuchhandlung, 1963.

KNIGHT, Everett. *A Theory of the Classical Novel*, London: Routledge and Kegan Paul, 1969.

188

KROEBER, Karl. *Romantic Narrative Art*, Madison: University of Wisconsin Press, 1960.

LALO, Charles. *L'expression de la vie dans l'art*, Paris: Alcon, 1933.

LEAVIS, F. R. *Revaluation: Tradition and Development in English Poetry*, New York: Stewart, 1947.

LECERCLE, Jean-Louis. *Rousseau et l'art du roman*, Paris: Librairie Armand Colin, 1969.

LEJEUNE, Philippe. *L'autobiographie en France*, Paris: Librairie Armand Colin, 1971.

LEVER, Katherine. *The Novel and the Reader*, London: Methuen & Co., Ltd., 1961.

LILLARD, Richard G. *American Life in Autobiography*, Stanford: Stanford University Press, 1956.

LINDENBERGER, Herbert. *On Wordsworth's Prelude*, Princeton: Princeton University Press, 1963.

LINDQUIST, Wilfred H. *Wordsworth's Prelude as an Autobiography*, unpublished Master Thesis, Minneapolis: University of Minnesota, 1941.

LOGAN, JORDAN & FRYE. *Some British Romantics*, Columbus: Ohio State University Press, 1966.

LUKACS, Georg. *Goethe and His Age*, New York: Grosset and Dunlap, 1969.

LYON, Judson. *The Excursion: A Study*, New Haven: Yale University Press, 1970.

- . - *Thomas De Quincey*, New York: Twayne Publishers, Inc., 1969.

MANN, Thomas. *Confessions of Felix Krull, Confidence Man*, tr. Denver Lindley, New York: The New American Library, Inc. 1963.

MASSON, David. *De Quincey,* New York: AMS Press, 1968 (reprint from the 1888 London edition).

MATTHEWS, William. *British Autobiographies*, Berkeley and Los Angeles: University of California Press, 1955.

MAUROIS, André. *The Art of Writing*, tr. Gerard Hopkins, London: The Bodley Head, 1960.

MAY, George. *Rousseau–par lui-même*, Paris: Editions du Seuil, 1961.

MEADOWS, Taylor. *The Confession of a Thug*, London and New York: Oxford University Press, 1916.

MEYER, Heinrich. *Goethe: Das Leben im Werk*, Stuttgart: Hans E. Gunther Verlag, 1967.

- . - *Die Kunst des Erzählens*, Bern: A. Francke Verlags-AG, 1972.

MILLER, J. Hillis, ed. *Aspects of the Narrative*, New York and London: Columbia University Press, 1971.

- . - *The Disappearance of God*, New York: Schocken Books, 1965.

MISCH, Georg. *Geschichte der Autobiographie*, 4 vol., Frankfurt/M.: G. Schulte-Bulmke Verlag, 1969.

MONK, Samuel H. *The Sublime: A Study of Critical Theories in XVIII Century England*, New York: Modern Language Association, 1935.

MONTAIGNE. *Oeuvres Complètes*, Paris: Gallimard, 1962.

MORRIS, John N. *Versions of the Self*, New York: Basic Books Inc., 1966.

MUGGERIDGE, Malcolm. *Chronicle of Wasted Time*, New York: Morrow, 1972.

MÜLLER, Günther. *Kleine Goethe Biographie*, 5th ed., Frankfurt/M.: Athenäum-Verlag, 1963.

MYRDAL, Jan. *The Confessions of a Disloyal European*, New York: Pantheon Books, 1968.

NADLER, Josef. *Franz Grillparzer*, Wien: Bergland Verlag, 1952.

NAUMANN, Walter. *Franz Grillparzer: Das dichterische Werk*, Stuttgart: W. Kohlhammer Verlag, 1967 (2. veränderte Aufl.).

O'CONNELL, Robert. *Saint Augustine's Confessions: The Odyssey of a Soul*, Cambridge, Mass.: The Belknap Press of Harvard University Press, 1969.

ONORATO, Richard. *The Character of the Poet: Wordsworth in the Prelude*, Princeton: Princeton University Press, 1971.

OSBORN, James M. *The Beginning of Autobiography in England*, Berkeley and Los Angeles: University of California Press, 1959.

OWEN, W. J. B. *Wordsworth as Critic*, Toronto: University of Toronto Press, 1969.

PASCAL, Roy. *Design and Truth in Autobiography*, Cambridge: Harvard University Press, 1960.

PECKHAM, Morse. *Beyond the Tragic Vision: The Quest for Identity in the Nineteenth Century*, New York: George Braziller, 1962.

PERKINS, David. *The Quest for Permanence*, Cambridge: Harvard University Press, 1959.

- . - *Wordsworth and the Poetry of Sincerity*, Cambridge: The Belknap Press of Harvard University Press, 1964.

PEYRE, Henri. *Literature and Sincerity*, Yale Romantic Studies, second series 9, New Haven and London: Yale University Press, 1963.

PHIPSON, Th. L. *The Confession of a Violinist*, London: Chatto & Windus, 1902.

PICHON, Jean Ch. *L'autobiographie*, Paris: Grasset, 1956.

PORTER, J. Roger. *The Voices Within*, New York: Alfred A. Knopf, 1973.

PROCTOR, Sigmund K. *Thomas De Quincey's Theory of Literature*, Ann Arbor: The University of Michigan Press, 1943.

PURKIS, John. *A Preface to Wordsworth*, London: Longman Group Ltd., 1970.

READ, Herbert. *Wordsworth*, New York: Jonathan Cape and Harrison Smith, 1931.

REICHENKRON, Günter, ed. *Formen der Selbstdarstellung*, Berlin: Duncker & Humblot, 1956.

RITCHIE, Paul. *The Confession of a People Lover*, London: Calder & Boyars, 1967.

RITTER, Eugene. *La Famille et la jeunesse de J.-J. Rousseau*, Paris: Hachette et Cie, 1896.

ROUSSEAU, Jean-Jacques. *Oeuvres—Les Confessions—autres textes autobiographiques*, vol. 1, ed. Gagnebin and Raymond, Paris: Gallimard, 1959.

-.- *Les Confessions*, Paris: Librairie Générale Française, 1963.

RUTTKOWSKI, Wolfgang V. *Die literarischen Gattungen*, Bern: A. Francke Verlags-AG., 1968.

SAINTE-BEUVE, C. A. *Portraits of the Eighteenth Century,* tr. K. P. Wormerly, New York, London: G. P. Putnam's Sons, 1905.

SAISSELIN, R. G. *Taste in Eighteenth Century France*, Syracuse: Syracuse University Press, 1965.

SALAMAN, Esther. *The Great Confession*, London: Allen Lane-The Penguin Press, 1973.

SANKO, Hélène. *La Question du beau dans la presse periodique française*, unpublished dissertation, Cleveland: Case Western Reserve University, 1971.

SAYRE, Robert F. *The Examined Self*, Princeton: Princeton University Press, 1964.

SCHOENBERNER, Franz. *The Confession of a European Intellectual*, New York: The Macmillan Company, 1946.

SCHREYVOGEL, Friedrich. *Franz Grillparzer—Dichter der letzten Dinge*, Wien: Stiasny Verlag, 1958.

SCHUMAKER, Wayne. *English Autobiography: Its Emergence, Material, and Form*, Berkeley and Los Angeles: University of California Press, 1954.

SCHÜTZ, Martin, ed. *Goethe Centenary Papers*, Chicago and London: The Open Court Publishing Company, 1933.

SIMPSON, Louis. *James Hogg: A Critical Study*, New York: St. Martin's Press, 1962.

SINGER, Godfrey F. *The Epistolary Novel*, New York: Russell & Russell, Inc., 1963.

SNOECK, A. S. J. *Confession and Pastoral Psychology*, Westminster: The Newman Press, 1961.

SPEIRS, John. *Poetry Towards Novel,* London: Faber & Faber, 1971.

SPRAGUE, Allen B. *Tides in English Taste 1619-1800*, Cambridge: Harvard University Press, 1937.

STAIGER, Emil. *Goethe*, 3 vol., Zürich: Atlantis Verlag, 1959.

STAROBINSKI, J. *Jean-Jacques Rousseau; La transparence et l'obstacle*, Paris: Gallimard, 1971.

STEKEL, Wilhelm. *Die Träume der Dichter*, Wiesbaden: J. F. Bergmann, 1912.

STYRON, William. *The Confession of Nat Turner*, New York: Random House, 1967.

THOMSON, A. W., ed. *Wordsworth's Mind and Art*, New York: Barnes and Noble, Inc., 1970.

VERLAINE, Paul. *Confessions d'un poète*, New York: Philosophical Library, 1950.

VIËTOR, Karl. *Goethe*, Bern: A. Francke Verlags-AG., 1949.

WELLEK, René. *Theory of Literature*, New York: Harcourt, Brace & Co., 1942.

WELLS, H. G. *Experiment in Autobiography*, New York: The MacMillan Company, 1934.

WEST, Edward. S. *Thomas De Quincey: His Life and Work*, New Haven: Yale University Press, 1936.

WETHERED, H. N. *The Curious Art of Autobiography*, London: Christopher Johnson, 1956.

WORDSWORTH, Christopher. *Memoirs of William Wordsworth*, Boston: Ticknor, Reed & Fields, 1851.

WORDSWORTH, Jonathan, ed. *Bicentenary Wordsworth Studies*, Ithaca and London: Cornell University Press, 1970.

WORDSWORTH, William. *The Prelude*, rev. ed., E. De Selincourt and Helen Darbyshire ed., London: Oxford University Press, 1960.

WORDSWORTH, William, *Early Letters of William and Dorothy*, ed. E. De Selincourt, Oxford: At the Clarendon Press, 1935.

-.-*Poetical Works*, ed. Th. Hutchinson, New York and London: Oxford University Press, 1967.

YUKIO, Mishima (pseud. Hiroaka Kimilte). *The Confession of a Mask*, tr. M. Weatherby, New York: New Directions, 1958.

ZALL, Paul, ed. *Literary Criticism of William Wordsworth*, Lincoln: University of Nebraska Press, 1966.

ARTICLES

AICHINGER, Ingrid. "Probleme der Autobiographie als Sprach-kunstwerk," *Österreichische Geschichte und Literatur*, XIV, 1970, pp. 418-434.

BENZINGER, James. "Organic Unity: Leibnitz to Coleridge," *PMLA*, LXVI, 1951, pp. 24-48.

CREMIEUX, Benjamin. "Sincerité et imagination," *Nouvelle Revue Française*, XII, 1924, pp. 528-548.

DARBYSHIRE, Helen. "Wordsworth's Belief in the Doctrine of Nec-essity," *Review English Studies,* XXIV, 1948, pp. 121-125.

DOBRÉE, Bonamy. "Some Literary Autobiographies of the Present Age," *Sewanee Review,* LXIV, Fall 1956, pp. 689-706.

HARVEY, J. "Content Characteristics of Best-selling Novels," *Tabs. Public Opinion Q.* XVII #1, 1953, pp. 91-114.

HEYER, Th. "Une inscription relative à J.-J. Rousseau," *Memoirs et Documents*, Société d'Histoire et d'Archéologie de Génève, IX, 1855, pp. 409-420.

IAN, Jack. "De Quincey Revises His Confessions," *PMLA*, LXXII, pp. 122-146.

JAMIESON, P. F. "Musset, De Quincey and Piranesi," *Modern Language Notes*, LXXI, Fall 1956, pp. 105-108.

JOST, François. "Le roman épistolaire et la téchnique narrative au XVIIIe siècle," *Comparative Literature*, III, 1966, pp. 397-427.

MANDEL, B. J. "The Autobiographer's Art," *Journal of Aesthetics and Art Criticism*, XXVI, Dec. 1968, pp. 215-216.

MORNET, Daniel. "Les enseignements des bibliothèques privées," *Revue d'Histoire Littéraire de la France*, XVII, 1910, pp. 449-496.

MUGGERIDGE, Malcolm. "Lives of Great Men All Remind Us," *The New Statesman and Nation*, June 1957, pp. 771-776.

REED, Mark. "The Speaker of the Prelude," *Bicentenary Words-worth Studies*, Ithaca and London: Cornell University Press, 1970.